TREASURES FROM THE PSALMS

ALSO BY HENRY GARIEPY

Devotional Study of the Names of Jesus (Fleming Revell, 1972)
Footsteps to Calvary (Fountain Press, 1977)
Study Guide: Footsteps to Calvary (Fountain Press, 1977)
Advent of Jesus Christ (Salvation Army USA Eastern Territory, 1979)
Study Guide: Advent of Jesus Christ (SA USA Eastern Territory, 1979)
100 Portraits of Christ (Victor Books, 1987)
Portraits of Perseverance – From the Book of Job (Victor Books 1989)
Christianity in Action – The Salvation Army in the USA Today (Victor Books, 1990)
Wisdom to Live By (Victor Books, 1991)
General of God's Army (Victor Books, 1993)
Challenge and Response – A Documentary on Christianity in Action (TSA, 1994)
40 Days with the Savior (Thomas Nelson Publishers, 1995)
Light in a Dark Place – From the Prophets (Victor Books, 1995)
Guidebook for Salvation Army Writers and Editors (TSA IHQ, 1995)
Healing in the Heartland (TSA Arkansas and Oklahoma Division, 1996)
Songs in the Night (William B. Eerdmans Publishing Co., 1996)
A Century of Service in Alaska (TSA Alaska Division, 1998)
Mobilized for God, International History of The Salvation Army, Volume 8
    (TSA IHQ, 2000)
A Salvationist Treasury (Crest Books, 2000)
Andy Miller – A Legend and a Legacy (TSA, 2002)
31 Days with God in Life's Trials and Testings (Cook Ministries, 2002)

CONTRIBUTOR TO:

Guidebook to Successful Christian Writing (TSA IHQ, 1996)
The Salvationist Pulpit (TSA USA East, 1991)
Discipleship (TSA Canada, 1995)
Encouragement in the Word (TSA Canada, 1995)
Genius of the New Testament Church (Charles W. Carter, 1995)
The Book of Jesus (Simon & Schuster, 1996)
The Christian Daily Planner (Word, 1996)
Count Your Blessings (Victor Books, 1997)
Christmas Through the Years (Crest Books, 1997)
The Hunger of Your Heart (Partnership Press, 1998)
Easter Through the Years (Crest Books, 1999)
Called By My Name (Partnership Press, 1999)
NIV Reflecting God Study Bible (Zondervan and CHP, 2000)
Essential Practices (Bristol Books, 2000)
A Pen of Flame (Crest Books, 2001)

Treasures from the Psalms

100 Meditations from the
Devotional Treasury of the Ages

Henry Gariepy

William B. Eerdmans Publishing Company
Grand Rapids, Michigan / Cambridge, U.K.

© 2002 Wm. B. Eerdmans Publishing Co.

Wm. B. Eerdmans Publishing Co.
255 Jefferson Ave. S.E., Grand Rapids, Michigan 49503 /
P.O. Box 163, Cambridge CB3 9PU U.K.
www.eerdmans.com

Printed in the United States of America

07 06 05 04 03 02   7 6 5 4 3 2 1

ISBN 0-8028-6081-8

To

Daughter Becky
Bud
Brian
Jennifer
Andrew

whose lives exemplify
the praise and prayers
of the Psalms

Contents

Introduction

> *Let the word of Christ dwell in you richly in all wisdom,*
> *teaching and admonishing one another in psalms.*
> (Col. 3:16, KJV)

FOR MANY, PSALMS IS the best-loved and most-quoted book of the Bible. The book of Psalms is the devotional treasury of the ages, its golden truths an unfailing resource for meditation, worship, praise, prayer, and song for the people of God.

The Bible, as a whole, is God's word to humankind. The Psalms echo human beings' words to God, their radiant truths forged in the testings and traumas of human experience. In the days and weeks following the unimaginable tragedy in our country on September 11, 2001, we heard the Psalms quoted over and over again. Psalm 46, read as the Bible text in the service attended by our nation's leaders in the National Cathedral, practically became the standard text for the expression of faith and courage throughout America.

This hymnbook of God's Word is read, recited, or sung every day. The message of the Psalter still resonates around the world in hymns based on its verses, such as the majestic strains of Martin Luther's "A Mighty Fortress Is Our God," Isaac Watts's "O God, Our Help in Ages Past," and a continuing spate of contemporary lyrics.

Psalms has more authors than any other book of the Bible, though the real author is, of course, the Holy Spirit. Seventy-three are ascribed to David, who had more diverse roles of life than any other person in Scripture. The Psalms cover a span of about 1,000 years, with Psalm 90 the oldest, written by Moses about 1,500 B.C., and Psalm 137 written at the end of the Babylonian exile, about 500 B.C. Only Genesis covers as long a period. Although ancient, their truths and inspiration are timeless, as up-to-date as tomorrow's newscast.

In the New Testament, no less than 116 of its 283 quotations from the Old Testament come from the Psalms. Jesus quoted from them more than from any other book, and to read them is to discover the prayer book of our Lord. The devout and serious reader of Psalms will take a Christocentric approach, for as Dietrich Bonhoeffer reminds us, "Christ is the secret of the Psalms."

Paul and Silas in prison at Philippi sang from the Psalms. The early church turned to the Psalms as the first Christian hymnbook. The Pilgrims chanted them as they crossed the sea to a new land in search of religious freedom. The first published book in America was the Pilgrim's Psalter.

Renowned Christians and Bible scholars present their striking eulogies. The fourth-century monk Athanasius declared: "Psalms are an epitome of the whole Scriptures." Augustine likened the Psalms to a school, saying: "What is there that may not be learned in the Psalms?" Ambrose provided a livelier metaphor, that of a "gymnasium," for a daily spiritual workout. Calvin testified: "Psalms is an anatomy of all the parts of the soul for there is not an emotion of which one can be conscious that is not here represented as in a mirror." Bible expositor Adam Clarke asserts: "Psalms is the most useful book in the Bible." Charles H. Spurgeon, in his monumental work on the Psalms, written over a period of twenty years, described them as "a theological anthology of the whole realm of Christian truth, infinities of truth flung into mere phrases, volumes of wisdom in single lines of poetry." He counseled: "He who would be wise, let him read the Proverbs; he that would be holy, let him read the Psalms." Billy Graham has made it a practice to read one chapter of Proverbs and five psalms every day, which takes him through these two books each month.

The psalms are unrelenting in their realism about the human psyche and holistic in insisting that the mundane and the holy are inextricably linked. They identify our deepest needs and articulate our heart's longings before God. In these poems we find loneliness, trial, sorrow, joy, rage, tragedy, fear, longing, penitence, praise, thanksgiving, and searching after God. In other words, we find ourselves.

The authors of the psalms crafted their compositions creatively. They were heirs of an ancient art, presenting to us the Psalter in Hebrew poetry, with its distinctive feature of parallelism. Most poetic lines are composed of two balanced segments. The second segment either echoes (synonymous parallelism), contrasts (antithetic parallelism), or completes (synthetic parallelism) the first. At the core of the theology of the Psalter is the conviction that the gravitational center of life, history, and the whole creation is "the Lord."

Praise and thanksgiving permeate the Psalms, with the word "praise" repeated 162 times in the paeans that scintillate throughout. The Psalms also is essentially a book on prayer, the best book on prayer ever composed. The Psalter is not only the prayer book in Hebrew history; it is also the enduring prayer book of the people of God. When we make the psalms our own, spiritually internalizing their longings and prayers, we enter into divine communion.

We come to this devotional treasury, not primarily as students to acquire knowledge, but as pilgrims to acquire a closer walk with God. May this volume lead us into the music rooms of the Psalms, where the Holy Spirit may play upon every chord of our human nature, as we discover anew the Psalms' transforming power and enrichment of our experience with God.

Heavenly Father, with the psalmist, I pray, "Open my eyes, that I may see wonderful things in your law."

CHAPTER 1

The Two Ways of Life

PSALM 1

> *Blessed is the man who walks not in the counsel of the ungodly.*
> (1:1a, NKJV)

PSALM 1 IS A SIGNPOST at the beginning. It points out and defines the two ways of life. Its teaching is a foundation for the whole book.

"Blessed" is the first word we encounter in the Psalms. What an appropriate introduction that word and this psalm are to the Psalter. The Psalms open with a benediction, pronouncing a blessing upon us as we enter, just as the Sermon on the Mount does.

This psalm first describes the righteous man. He is "blessed." He has joy in his fellowship and experience with God. The man or woman of God is a happy person. We are not to endure but to enjoy our religion.

The Hebrew word used here for blessed is plural, representing the multiplicity of blessings we have from God. Our blessings from God are innumerable and incredibly diverse.

The righteous person forsakes and shuns evil. He does not "walk . . . stand . . . or sit" in the way of sin (v. 1). It may be difficult for us to avoid the "counsel of the ungodly" in our secular society. Circumstances often compel believers to associate with non-Christians, sometimes at work, in business, perhaps even in the home. And today, who can escape the influence of the all-

1

pervasive, and sometimes subliminally persuasive, television screen? But while Christians must be in the world, they are not of the world. They do not heed the ungodly influences nor indulge in the habits and lifestyles of sin around them.

What we enjoy provides an index to our character. What is our attitude toward the Bible? Is it a source of enjoyment for us? Of the man of God the psalmist says, "But his delight is in the law of the LORD" (v. 2). The psalmist found pleasure in reading and meditating on God's "law," which in his day consisted of the first five books of Moses, just a fragment of the treasury of God's Word that has come down to us. If the psalmist took delight in such a fragmentary record, how much greater should be our enthusiasm for the divine record of both the Old and New Testament. For the Christian, the reading and study of the Bible are not drudgery but a delight.

The godly man is "like a tree planted" (v. 3). His life is fixed; it is stable. Roots plunged deep into the soil of prayer and devotion nourish his life so that he can withstand the winds and storms that will surely come.

"He is like a tree planted by streams of water, which yields its fruit in season" (v. 3). Each tree has its unique function. Ash wood is used for tennis rackets, baseball bats, and oars; beech trees produce food for wildlife; hickory is best for fire logs with its long burning, clean ash, and beautiful flame. Poplar seeds germinate with alacrity in burned forests. Bald cypress wood, which is almost decay proof, is used for coffins and shingles. Trees – and people – have a purpose for being.

Every life is a fresh thought from the mind of God. No two stars, no two snowflakes, no two fingerprints, no two lives are the same. Each person has a purpose no other can fulfill. Our Lord needed Peter's unpolished frankness, Andrew's natural friendliness, Thomas's questing and scientific mind, Paul's schoolroom learning, and Matthew's gift of penmanship and detail. He needs the unique gift that each of us can bring to the work of his kingdom.

The righteous man is not only like a fruit-bearing tree, but also like a tree "whose leaf does not wither" (v. 3). He is as an evergreen, unchanging in his freshness and joy in the things of God.

Psalm 1 is a study in contrasts. It depicts the righteous man in contrast to the ungodly, the wheat as opposed to the chaff, and the dramatic climax of the two ways of life. It points to the path of life that leads to our true destiny.

Help me, Lord, at the crossroads of life, to choose your way and thereby find my destiny.

CHAPTER 2

The Ultimate Choice

Psalm 1, Continued

> *The way of the wicked will perish.*
> (1:6b)

IN THE FIRST PART of Psalm 1, the psalmist characterizes the righteous man as blessed of God, having a fondness for the law of God and a life that is fixed and fruitful. The ungodly man is portrayed as just the opposite.

The psalmist cites three steps in the downward spiral to destruction. First, the ungodly man *walks* in the way of sin. Sin gets his attention. He entertains sinful ideas. He starts to keep company with sin. Second, he *stands* in sin. Standing is a more settled posture than walking. There is now no movement away from sin but a settling in. Finally, he *sits*. He becomes habituated to evil.

Augustine, writing in his *Confessions* of his bondage to sin prior to conversion, warns of this downward spiral of sin: "A perverse will produces lust. Lust yielded to becomes a habit. A habit not resisted becomes a necessity. These were like links of a chain hanging one upon the other, and they bound me hand and foot."

The ungodly "are like chaff that the wind blows away" (v. 4). Farmers winnowed grain by throwing it up into the air with three-pronged forks. The wind blew away the chaff, the useless part of the grain. The ungodly are thus portrayed as purposeless and unstable. Their end is destruction.

The psalm concludes with the words, "the way of the wicked will perish" (v. 6). Charles H. Spurgeon put it memorably: "The righteous carves his name upon the rock, but the wicked writes his remembrance in the sand."

This introduction to the Psalter, with its graphic teaching on the two ways of life, is underscored by the teachings of Christ himself. Our Lord also spoke graphically about the two ways of life: "Enter through the narrow gate. For wide is the gate and broad is the road that leads to destruction, and many enter through it. But small is the gate and narrow the road that leads to life, and only a few find it" (Matthew 7:13-14).

For the sinner, Psalm 1 serves as a call to repentance. For the

Christian it is a call to renewal to assure that we remain on the straight and narrow path that leads to life eternal.

Those who travel across the heartland of America encounter the Continental Divide, where two raindrops falling inches apart can end up in different oceans. Our text speaks of a great spiritual divide, one side leading to destruction, the other to everlasting life.

The words of John Oxenham are like a glove thrown at our feet:

> *To every man there openeth*
> *A way, and ways, and a way.*
> *And the high soul climbs the high way,*
> *And the low soul gropes the low,*
> *And in between, on the misty flats,*
> *The rest drift to and fro.*
> *But to every man there openeth*
> *A high way and a low, and every man decideth*
> *The way his soul shall go.*

An exhibit of relics from the *Titanic* touring the country brought to life images of that ship's memorably tragic disaster. Exhibit visitors received a replica ticket, containing the name of an actual passenger or crew member, a reminder that the exhibit was about real people. At the end of the tour a large board listed the names of all the people who had been aboard, along with their categories – First Class, Second Class, Third Class, and Crew. The names were listed in two columns, "Saved" or "Lost." The parallel to our life is profound. It doesn't matter which class we are traveling; the only thing that ultimately matters at the end of the voyage is whether we are "Saved" or "Lost."

Many adopt as their theme the sentiment of the popular song, "I did it my way." Spiritually, as this psalm warns in its last word, "perish," our way apart from God leads to destruction. Let our theme song for life be instead, "I did it God's way." Only then do we find the true meaning of life and realize its God-given destiny.

Lord, we look to you as the Way – the way to salvation, to purposeful living, and to life eternal.

CHAPTER 3

Our Rebel World

PSALM 2

> *Why do the nations rage*
> *and the peoples plot in vain?*
> (2:1)

PSALM 1 DEALS WITH the individual; Psalm 2 deals with the world. The first psalm relates to our personal life, the second to our corporate life. Both are in the plan and purpose of God.

Psalm 2 portrays a tumultuous scene – armies marching, anarchy, revolt. It describes a rebel world and God's derision, deliverance, and decree. It is a wide-angle lens on humanity.

"Why do the nations rage?" This statement mirrors our

world torn by international tensions, violence, terrorism, and the ominous threat of a biological or nuclear holocaust. If God is sovereign over history, why this rebellion? If he is the God of order and harmony, why this chaos and anarchy?

"The peoples plot in vain" (2:1b). Many today are under the spell of horoscopes, eastern mysticism, or cultism. Our culture promotes same-sex marriage, creative divorce, and relativism rather than absolutism in values. Our world is in rebellion against the laws and moral standards of God.

Psalm 2 is the first messianic psalm; verse 2 gives us the first reference to Christ in the Psalms, describing the rulers of the earth taking counsel against "his Anointed One." This word *anointed* is *Messiah* in Hebrew and *Christ* in Greek.

"'Let us break their chains,' they say, 'and throw off their fetters'" (v. 3). Here is the reason for the disorder in the world. It is the rebellious will of humankind speaking, in opposition to the moral authority of God. The rebel says, "Let us rid ourselves of restraint, let us be free to do as we want." He demands license in place of liberty. He echoes the lost archangel's words in Milton's *Paradise Lost:* "Better to reign in hell than serve in heaven."

Then follows the terrifying scene of the laughter of God (v. 4). Sin, a rebellion against God, can produce the scornful laughter of the One enthroned in heaven. But we must remember that the wrath of God is always intertwined with love on the death beams of the cross.

Amid all this fury and anarchy, God intervenes. He inaugurates a new age with a covenant relationship. He declares his unique relationship with his anointed: "You are my Son" (v. 7). Paul in his preaching relates this very verse and statement to the resurrection of Christ (Acts 13:33), which will enthrone him as the redeemer and sovereign of the world. Hebrews 1:5 also cites this text to emphasize the supremacy of Christ.

God also decreed the ultimate, worldwide authority of Christ: "I will make the nations your inheritance, the ends of the earth your possession" (v. 8). The penman of Patmos sees this decree fulfilled in the final triumph of Christ's kingdom (Revelation 2:26-27).

God's word to the nations is: "Be wise . . . Serve the LORD . . . Kiss the Son, lest he be angry, and you be destroyed" (vv. 10-12). To "kiss the Son" is an act of homage and devotion. The wisdom of a nation, as well as an individual, is found in homage to Christ and his principles of righteousness and justice.

The conclusion of this psalm takes us from the ragings of the world and the storms of self-will to the peace of God, with the beatitude: "Blessed are all who take refuge in him" (v. 12). The burden of this evangelistic psalm is for God to lead us from rebellion to redemption, from chaos to Christ.

G. K. Chesterton reflects the message of this psalm:

> O God of earth and altar,
> Bow down and hear our cry;
> Our earthly rulers falter,
> Our people drift and die;
> The walls of gold entomb us,
> The swords of scorn divide,
> Take not thy thunder from us,
> But take away our pride.

Our Father, lead us in the way of peace.

CHAPTER 4

An Evening Prayer

PSALM 4

> *I will lie down and sleep in peace.*
>
> (4:8)

PSALMS IS ESSENTIALLY A book of prayer. Prayer should be the key of the morning and the bolt of the night. In Psalms 4 and 5 we have an evening and a morning prayer, as the psalmist prayed at both ends of the day. He both closed and began the day with God.

Psalm 4 introduces the ascription, "For the director of music," which appears at the beginning of fifty-four psalms. (The King James Version renders it "To the Chief Musician.") The meaning is obscure, but it underscores the prominent role of music in worship and devotion in the psalmist's day.

Music is one of the most beautiful gifts of God to humankind. Words are the pen of the heart, but music is the pen of the soul. Often God speaks with his clearest accents through the strains of sacred song or an instrument played to his glory. Music, so powerful a carrier of thoughts too unearthly to be fully expressed, elevates the soul to heights of communion with God. Through the centuries, devotional music consistently called from the great composers their highest artistic achievements, and many of the psalms are the progeny of prayer and worship set to music.

Three men occupied the position of chief musician under

David: Asaph, Heman, and Jeduthun. We read that in Heman's house there were fourteen sons and three daughters, and their entire household was "under the direction of their father for music in the house of the LORD, with cymbals, stringed instruments, and harps, for the service of the house of God" (1 Chronicles 25:5-6, NKJV). There was an entire symphony in his house!

We first encounter in this psalm the word "selah" (v. 2), found seventy-three times in thirty-nine psalms and three times in the third chapter of Habakkuk. The common suggestion is that this word indicated a pause, a notation to stop, ponder, and meditate. We would do well to pause, and meditate, as we come upon the timeless and sublime truths in the Psalms.

The psalmist enjoins us: "When you are on your beds, search your hearts and be silent" (v. 4b). Psychologists tell us that the last thoughts of the day seep into our subconscious and become an important part of our psyche. How salutary it is for the soul, then, to meditate upon the things of God at the end of the day, to close the day with God.

How do we end our day? Too many today allow their last minutes to be dominated by the television screen with its offerings of sex and violence, or scenes that bring distress to the psyche.

The psalmist invites us away from our sound-soaked world to what Thomas Kelly termed "the recreating silences." Silent meditation is still a gateway to the presence of God. Francis de Sales (1567-1622) in *The Devout Life* counsels, "There is an art to making the transition from prayer to earning a living. When your silent prayer is over, remain still and quiet for a few moments. Make your transition to other responsibilities gradually. Linger yet a while in the garden. Walk carefully along the path so that you won't spill the precious balm you are carrying."

The psalmist himself was not without his troubles and tribulations. In the preceding psalm he cries out, "O Lord, how many are my foes! How many rise up against me!" (3:1). But the psalmist's antidote to trouble is trust. His trust in God brought peace. Because of his evening communion, he could say, "I will lie down and sleep in peace" (4:8).

Sleep is the gift of God. He bids the sun to close its eyes, draws down the curtain of darkness, rocks the cradle for the world each night, and bids us slumber that our bodies may be refreshed for tomorrow's toil. How thankful we should be for God's gift of sleep. It's the best physician, having healed more pains and sicknesses than the best doctors. A clear conscience lulls the soul to sleep.

Many suffer from insomnia and restlessness and require sleeping pills to get a night's sleep. But the psalmist knew that a good conscience is a soft pillow and a quiet bedfellow. He found rest in his waiting upon God. By the end of the day tensions may build up like barnacles on a cruise ship. Ending the day with God helps remove the incrustations and brings a restful peace.

This evening hymn of the psalmist advises us: when you can't sleep, don't count sheep. Talk to the Shepherd.

Prince of Peace, at the end of the day give to me a quiet heart of communion and trust.

CHAPTER 5

A Morning Meditation

PSALM 5

> *Morning by morning, O LORD, you hear my voice;*
> *morning by morning I lay my requests before you*
> *and wait in expectation.*
>
> (5:3)

C. S. LEWIS, IN HIS book *The Screwtape Letters,* introduces Screwtape, a demon in the upper echelons of hellish status. The book is a collection of Screwtape's letters to his nephew Wormwood, a novice demon, advising him how to defeat Christians in the battle of life. He warns in relation to prayer, "Interfere at any price in any fashion when people start to pray, for real prayer is lethal to our cause."

Indeed, prayer holds the secret to growth and victory in the Christian life. The psalms are saturated with prayer; indeed, many of them are prayers, including Psalm 5. In the Hebrew tradition, the day began at sundown. The creation account reads, "There was evening, and there was morning – the first day" (Genesis 1:5). Thus it is apt that Psalm 5, a morning meditation, follows Psalm 4, an evening prayer.

There is a spiritual energy and urgency to the opening of this psalm: "Give ear to my words, O LORD, consider my sighing. Listen to my cry for help" (vv. 1-2). This prayer is charged with spiritual fervency.

The psalmist believed in starting his day with God:

Morning by morning, O LORD, you hear my voice;
morning by morning I lay my requests before you
and wait in expectation.   (v. 3)

This double reference to "morning by morning" underscores the importance of the thought. The person who gives his first waking thoughts to God will be more disposed to walk with God throughout the day. As the grass and flowers in the morning are refreshed by the dew that comes before dawn quietly from above, so the soul that waits upon God in the first hour of the day is refreshed and nourished by the heavenly dews of God's grace.

Ralph S. Cushman has expressed it memorably in his poem, "The Secret":

I met God in the morning
  When the day was at its best,
And his presence came like sunrise,
  Like a glory in my breast.

All day long the presence lingered,
  All day long He stayed with me,
And we sailed in perfect calmness
  O'er a very troubled sea.

So I think I know the secret,
  Learned from many a troubled way;
You must seek Him in the morning
  If you want Him through the day.

We have Jesus' own example of morning prayer: "Very early in the morning, while it was still dark, Jesus got up, left the house and went off to a solitary place, where he prayed" (Mark 1:35). May we, in the freshness of the morning hour, commune with the Presence who will give strength and guidance throughout the day.

Francis de Sales advises that we "Sprinkle a seasoning of short prayers on our daily living. If you see something beautiful, thank God for it. If you are aware of someone's need, ask God to help. You can toss up many prayers all day long. Make a habit of it."

Nothing is more essential for the Christian, or more neglected, than prayer. Many devout believers are never fully satisfied with the quality of their prayer life. They may not be excited about praying, often find it a tiring ritual, and like to keep it as short as possible. Prayer and Bible reading can all too easily be caught up in the "fast food" syndrome of our day.

We need to take time to be holy, to nourish our souls in the Word and in divine communion. The practice and improvement of our prayer life is one of the greatest disciplines of the spiritual life. Our enrollment in the school of prayer is a lifetime undertaking.

Lord, "whose glory gilds the morning skies," help me start each day in your radiant presence.

CHAPTER 6

The Song of the Astronomer

PSALM 8

> O LORD, *our Lord,*
> *how majestic is your name in all the earth!*
> (8:1)

PSALM 8 HAS BEEN called "the song of the astronomer." A masterpiece among the psalms, enclosed in doxologies (vv. 1, 9), its elegant language proclaims the inexpressible theme of the glory of God.

Immanuel Kant affirmed: "Two things fill the mind with ever new and increasing awe and wonder – the starry heavens above me and the moral law within me." We so easily take for granted the stupendous wonders God has created with such abundance all around us. Were the stars to appear but once in a decade or a century, it would be occasion for a grand celebration.

Do you recall some moment of awe and wonder when you beheld the majesty and magnificence of a star-spangled sky? One such moment is enshrined in our family archives of memory. On a camping trip in northern Canada, after the evening campfire had died down, we strolled down to the lakeside, sat on some large rocks, and gazed up at the star-studded canopy of the heavens. It was one of those clear, moonless nights, so that the stars shone in all their resplendent beauty. I'll never forget the spontaneous exclamation of awe by our son, then about seven years of age. In a reverent tone of voice he said, "I never

15

knew there were so many stars!" It was a moment of prized and precious discovery.

In our highly urbanized world it is all too easy to miss the marvels of God's handiwork around us and to fail to ponder their majesty and meaning. A new urban generation may suppose that breakfast comes from the supermarket, heat from the furnace, and water from the spigot. In the devolution of things, grandfather had a farm, his son a garden, and his grandson a can opener! But the lifestyle of the shepherd who composed this psalm was one close to the wonders of nature.

On one dark, clear night, the shepherd of the psalms looked up at the star-bejeweled sky. The vast host of heavenly lights stretching from horizon to horizon erased from his mind the clutter of everyday affairs and engaged his mind with celestial thoughts. His spirit overflowed with awe and wonder. A burning of the poet kindled within him: "Where is my pen? I must write." A surge of music stirred in his soul: "Where is my harp? I must play."

The moment seemed inexpressible. He could only begin with an exclamation, addressed to God himself: "O LORD, our Lord, how majestic is your name in all the earth! You have set your glory above the heavens!" David's hillside song of praise that night became a classic of devotion for the ages.

The naked eye of the psalmist could not see more than some five thousand stars on a clear night. What would the psalmist have said if he could have peered out into fathomless space through one of our giant telescopes and discovered with the astronomers that the universe is made up of billions of galaxies, each containing, on average, a hundred billion stars! If he was struck with awe at the beauty and immensity of what he could see, how much more should we marvel in light of what modern astronomy reveals? We, even more than the psalmist, should exclaim, "O LORD, our Lord, how majestic is your name in all the earth!"

"When I consider your heavens," exclaimed the psalmist. Isaac Newton, one of the greatest scientific geniuses, when asked how he made such astonishing discoveries replied simply, "By thinking upon them." What exciting and profitable discoveries might we make by considering, by thinking about, God's marvelous creation and his handiwork all around us.

The psalmist properly terms the cosmos "*your* heavens." He saw beyond nature's grandeur to nature's Author, beyond earthly transience to eternal verities.

"Take a good look at God's wonders – they'll take your breath away" (Eugene Peterson's paraphrase of Psalm 66:5). When we consider God's creation of the cosmos, with all its mind-boggling wonders, we too are led to praise and adoration because of the transcendent greatness of God. With a modern-day psalmist we exultantly sing:

> *O Lord my God, when I in awesome wonder*
> *Consider all the worlds thy hands have made;*
> *I see the stars, I hear the rolling thunder,*
> *Thy power throughout the universe displayed;*
> *Then sings my soul, my Savior God to Thee;*
> *How great Thou art! How great Thou art!*

> (Carl G. Boberg, 1885; trans. Stuart K. Hine)

Heavenly Father, I praise you for your greatness, your goodness, and your glory.

CHAPTER 7

What Is Man?

Psalm 8, Continued

> *What is man that you are mindful of him?*
> (8:4)

"From the lips of children and infants" (v. 2) the Lord speaks to us. Our children may well be our greatest tutors. We learn from them what no university can begin to teach. Children's openness and limber imaginations can often more readily perceive spiritual truth. They instruct us in the deeper lessons of life – love, forgiveness, tenderness, caring, sacrifice, trust, acceptance.

Jesus said, "Unless you . . . and become like little children, you will never enter the kingdom of heaven" (Matthew 18:3). We need the childlike qualities of simple trust, spontaneous joy, natural response to beauty and truth, and uncalculated affection.

The psalmist moves on from his wonder at infants to ponder the status of humankind, of himself, in relation to the Creator. Awed at the incalculable grandeur of God as revealed in the heavens, he is moved to exclaim, "What is man that you are mindful of him?" (v. 4). Well might we ask, Is it credible that the Creator of this stupendous universe, with billions of galaxies and hundreds of billions of titanic stars, really knows and cares for me, such an infinitesimal speck in the vast universe?

The psalmist leads us to ponder our own identity, who we really are, from the viewpoint of God's glory in the world. What am I in relation to the fathomless cosmos? How do I fit into God's plan of creation? Why should the God of the universe be mindful of me? The psalmist's contemplation issues forth in his probing, pertinent, and provocative question: "What is man?" Who and what are we, really?

It is, of course, an ancient question. From time immemorial, people have discoursed on it. This query of the heart is old and quenchless. It is also an anxious question. Curiosity about the meaning of life holds a strange mixture of fear and hope. It is also an argued question. It has bred endless speculations and controversies. Bertrand Russell has called humankind "a curious accident." H. L. Mencken denigrates the human species: "Man is a parasite infecting the epidermis of a midget planet." Shakespeare's Macbeth decried: "Life's but a walking shadow."

The psalmist has one more thing to say about this seminal question he has posed. Ancient, anxious, and often argued, it is also an answered question. The psalmist portrays humanity as the crown of God's creation: "You made him a little lower than the heavenly beings and crowned him with glory and honor" (v. 5). He goes on to describe sublimely humankind's dominion over God's creation: "You made him ruler over the works of your hands; you put everything under his feet" (v. 6).

William Barclay describes this text as "the paradox of man. Frail, puny, transient, insignificant, mortal, but God has appointed him his viceroy on earth. . . . It is a dominion which man must be wise enough to use. . . . Dominion and obedience must go hand in hand."

God has spoken to humankind, telling us how much he does care for us. He has spoken through his living Word, through the cross, through the resurrection, and through his Spirit in our lives and in the world today.

You and I are Somebody in the plan and purpose of God. "Our dignity is that we are children of God," writes William Temple, "capable of communion with God, and destined for eternal fellowship with God." We are more than a restless protoplasm, enchanted dust, a fortuitous concourse of atoms, the plaything of an inscrutable fate, a pawn in the universe. Think of it, you and I are created "a little lower than the heavenly beings."

John Muir, renowned conservationist, signed his travel journal, "John Muir, Earth-planet, Universe." The psalmist here reminds us that we are indeed a part of God's purpose in his universe, that in the grand scheme of God we have a destiny beyond that of mere earthlings.

In Christ, human beings discover and become what God created them to be, made after God's own image, in the likeness of his love and holiness, and destined to eternal life. With Catherine Arnott, a psalmist of our day, we would praise and pray:

> God Who stretched the spangled heavens
> > Infinite in time and place,
> Flung the suns in burning radiance
> > Through the silent fields of space,
> We, Thy children, in Thy likeness,
> > Share inventive powers with Thee –
> Great Creator, still creating,
> > Teach us what we yet may be.

God of the galaxies, I praise and thank you for the eternal worth of my soul.

CHAPTER 8

A Delightful Inheritance

PSALM 16

> *Surely I have a delightful inheritance.*
> (16:6b)

THE PSALMIST, IN CONTEMPLATING how richly God has blessed his life, reminisces: "The boundary lines have fallen for me in pleasant places; surely I have a delightful inheritance" (v. 6). The metaphor is borrowed from the experience of the Israelites when they settled in Canaan. Each man or tribe received his inheritance or land portion by lot, bounded in by lines (Joshua 14:1-5). It represented, literally, his "lot" in life.

We too reflect upon the blessings that have come to us, not by our own doing, but by what has been our spiritual "lot" in life. For some there is the goodly heritage of Christian family and home. There is the heritage of our church, its teachings, worship, and fellowship. There is the heritage of God's Word, our salvation, our Lord himself, and the Holy Spirit. The psalmist exclaimed with exhilaration, "Surely I have a delightful inheritance."

The psalmist refers to the "night seasons" (v. 7, NKJV) as a time of instruction from God. The "night seasons" can represent times of trial and trouble. God enables us to testify with the psalmist, "I will praise the LORD, who counsels me. . . . Because he is at my right hand, I will not be shaken. Therefore my heart is glad" (vv. 7-9). When our trust is in the Lord, he turns our stresses into strengths, our pains into gains, and our brokenness into blessings.

In the midst of this psalm we suddenly come upon its radiant declaration: "You will not abandon me to the grave, nor will you let your Holy One see decay" (v. 10). Peter, on the day of Pentecost, quoted this verse as prophecy fulfilled in the resurrection of Christ (Acts 2:27-28). None other than our Lord is "your Holy One" who did not suffer decay. His body expired, but it never came to corruption. This messianic verse also has the latent promise that because Christ rose, we too can live forever.

The doctrine of the resurrection of the dead is a doctrine peculiar to Christianity. Nature, as well as God's Word, proclaims its glorious truth. A minute kernel of corn is buried, and not long afterward a green blade pierces the soil, growing finally to a stalk more than six feet tall and producing a hundredfold number of kernels. Or an acorn, weighing much less than an ounce, falls into the earth, and through the miracle of a resurrection springs up and produces a magnificent oak tree weighing more than two tons. If God deigns to bring forth such a resurrection from a small seed, shall he not do even more for his children created in and restored to his image? Through the seasons of this life we must endure the stern decree, "Dust to dust, earth to earth, ashes to ashes," but in the springtime of our soul every part of our being will exclaim, "Immortality!" The chrysalis shall fall off, and a new creation shall emerge.

Our country was traumatized by the ill-fated launch of spacecraft *Challenger* on January 28, 1986. The soul of our nation was seared as we saw the feathery flame explode the spacecraft and our courageous astronauts vanish in the fiery nightmare. Aboard was schoolteacher Christa McAuliffe, who had caught the imagination and won the heart of America. She ventured toward the heavens with her son's stuffed frog, her daughter's cross, her grandmother's watch, and a copy of the poem "High Flight." The poem was written by John Gillespie Magee, Jr., a young American volunteer with the Royal Canadian Air Force, who died over Britain in 1941. It was quoted by President Reagan as part of his eulogy for the astronauts:

> *Oh, I have slipped the surly bonds of earth . . .*
> *I've topped the wind-swept heights with easy grace,*
> *Where never lark, or even eagle, flew;*
> *And, while with silent, lifting mind I've trod*
> *The high, untrespassed sanctity of space,*
> *Put out my hand, and touched the face of God.*

The noble and ultimate heritage of the believer is to "slip the surly bonds of earth" and to come into the very presence of God.

Heavenly Father, I thank and praise you for the incredibly rich inheritance you give to us.

CHAPTER 9

Joy on the Journey

PSALM 16, CONTINUED

> *You have made known to me the path of life.*
> (16:11)

THE WORD *miktam* at the beginning of this psalm is considered to mean "golden." For many of God's people, this has been a "golden psalm," precious in its timeless truth and promise. It speaks to us of the path of life to which God beckons us.

Life is a journey, a path we are destined to walk. It has hidden pitfalls and perils. We are weak, frail, vulnerable. We need a guide who knows the way and can preserve us on our journey. The psalmist speaks for himself and all of us: "You have made known to me the path of life." What a blessed assurance that we need not be lost on life's journey, but that we have been shown the way that leads to life, both here and hereafter.

The two disciples of the Emmaus Road remind us that our Lord not only shows us the path of life but also journeys with us. How reassuring it is that we need not walk life's path alone. We too can know his radiant presence and belong to "the order of the burning heart." He will walk beside us and flood our prosaic paths with his peerless glory.

Bernard of Clairvaux, whose twelfth-century writings ushered in the golden age of medieval spirituality, wrote of his sense of God's presence: "How did I know He was in me? I couldn't miss it! My heart was softened and my soul roused

from its slumber. He went to work in me. He cleared and culti-
vated the soil of my soul. He planted and watered and brought
light to dark places. He opened what was closed, and warmed
what was cold. I have seen a fraction of his glory and it is awesome."

In the classic lines of Henry Lyte's hymn, we affirm our dependence on the Savior:

> *Abide with me, fast falls the eventide;*
> *The darkness deepens; Lord, with me abide!*
> *When other helpers fail, and comforts flee,*
> *Help of the helpless, O abide with me!*
>
> *Swift to its close ebbs out life's little day;*
> *Earth's joys grow dim, its glories fade away;*
> *Change and decay in all around I see;*
> *O thou who changest not, abide with me!*
>
> *I need thy presence every passing hour;*
> *What but thy grace can foil the tempter's power?*
> *Who like thyself my guide and stay can be?*
> *Through cloud and sunshine, O abide with me!*

(1847)

In one of the exhilarating testimonies of Scripture, the
psalmist affirms: "You will fill me with joy in your presence,
with eternal pleasures at your right hand" (11:b). What we know
of God's promise of joy is small compared with what we do not
know. The sea of his wisdom has cast up a few shells upon our
shore, but its vast depths will never be known until we enter
into the eternal joys prepared for us. In answer to the Anglican

catechism's question, "What is the chief end of man?" we are re-minded that it is "to glorify God, and to enjoy him forever." During and at the end of the path of life there is not just joy but "fullness of joy," and pleasures that will never fade, nor be inter-rupted, nor die. No wonder the psalmist exclaimed, "I have a de-lightful inheritance!"

As with the psalmist, we can confidently journey on our path of life, knowing that we have an all-knowing, unerring, and loving Guide.

Lord, you who are the Way, lead me safely on my path of life.

CHAPTER 10

Leaping Over Walls

PSALM 18

> *With my God I can scale a wall.*
> (18:29)

THE PSALMIST looks back, reflecting on the many dangers he has passed through and God's great deliverance in his life. In so doing, David, "the sweet psalmist of Israel," composes this hal-lelujah psalm to the God who enabled him to "leap over a wall." This psalm is so precious in the Bible that it is repeated, all fifty verses, in 2 Samuel 22.

One of our daughters each time she calls us on the phone always ends the conversation with, "I love you Mom, I love you Dad." To those nearest and dearest to us, we want to express time and again our love for them. This great psalm opens with just such a greeting to our heavenly Father: "I love you, O LORD, my strength." What more beautiful opening could there be to this psalm of praise than this affirmation of love for God? Do we tell God that we love him? Do we look back at all he has done for us and say, "I love you, Lord"?

Jesus taught that love for God is the first and greatest of the divine commandments (Mark 12:30). It is the "first" commandment, older than even the Ten Commandments. Before God said to humankind, "Thou shalt not commit adultery, Thou shalt not steal," this was a command in the universe, binding upon the angels. It was binding upon Adam and Eve in the Garden of Eden. "Love the Lord your God" is the king of commandments, taking precedence over all other requirements of human beings to their God. In his declaration of this as the greatest commandment, Jesus four times repeated the word "all." We are to love God with *all* our heart, with *all* our soul, with *all* our intellect, and with *all* our strength. This is the sum and substance of all the law of God. May we, with the psalmist of old, affirm our devotion, saying, "I love you, O LORD."

"The LORD is my rock," says David, as with a thankful heart he acknowledges that God had been to him his impregnable rock of safety from his enemies. More modern psalmists, the hymn writers, have also used this metaphor of a rock to represent the security of the believer and God's deliverance. Elizabeth Clephane described the cross as "the shadow of a mighty rock within a weary land." Fanny Crosby affirms for us all, "He hideth my soul in the cleft of the rock." Another modern psalmist, Edward Mote, versified, "On Christ, the solid Rock, I stand." And who has not sung with assurance these words by A. M. Toplady: "Rock of ages, cleft for me, let me hide myself in thee"?

Verses 4 and 5 of this psalm describe in vivid imagery the terrors and trials of David's past life: "The cords of death entangled me; the torrents of destruction overwhelmed me. The cords of the grave coiled around me; the snares of death confronted me." Francis Bacon expressed it memorably: "If you listen to David's harp, you shall hear as many hearse-like airs as carols; and the pencil of the Holy Spirit labored more in describing the afflictions of Job than the felicities of Solomon. We see, in needlework and embroideries, it is more pleasing to have a lively work upon a sad and solemn ground. Certainly virtue is like precious odors – most fragrant when crushed." The beauty of this psalm is enhanced against the dark background of dangers. Its fragrance is poured from a soul that knew the crushing. Should we not also express our love to God in grateful remembrance for his providence and deliverance amid the spiritual difficulties and dangers through which he has brought us?

This psalm describes the workings of God in striking metaphors (vv. 7-19). He is the God who "soared on the wings of the wind" (v. 10), "reached down from on high and took hold of me; he drew me out of deep waters" (v. 16). God also "turns my darkness into light" (v. 28).

Exhilaration leaps from the page as the psalmist exclaims: "With my God I can scale a wall" (v. 29). What walls arise in front of you? What blocks your escape from the enemy of your soul? What obstacle prevents you from becoming all God would have you be? You cannot scale that wall yourself. But, by God's power, you can "leap" over it and scale the walls of seeming impossibilities. God gives that exuberant victory when we surrender to him.

The psalmist further testifies, "He makes my feet like the feet of a deer" (v. 33). The psalmist had seen the surefooted deer scale the most precipitous rocks and swiftly outdistance its pursuing enemies. God orders with strength and security the steps of the believer. He enables us to go safely through the most perilous paths of life.

God, our strength, we praise you for your deliverance from Satan and sin and death.

CHAPTER 11

The World Book of God

PSALM 19

> *The heavens declare the glory of God;*
> *the skies proclaim the work of his hands.*
> (19:1)

IN THIS, ONE OF the most eloquent, indeed peerless poems of the Bible, the psalmist rhapsodizes about the World of God, the Word of God, and the Way of God. C. S. Lewis called Psalm 19 "the greatest poem in the Psalter and one of the greatest lyrics in the world."

"The heavens declare the glory of God" (v. 1a). The language of the heavens is not the noisy language of human beings. There is silence in the sunrise, a stillness to the stars. Yet they still speak eloquently of their Creator. God has written his autograph upon the sapphire parchment and across the velvet scroll of the night sky. The resplendent beauty and the pageantry of the heavens "proclaim the work of his hands" (v. 1b).

Not only the magnificent beauty of the heavens but also the precision and orderliness of the cosmos speak of God. If just one star would veer off course, that would make incredible news. The unerring precision of the heavenly bodies enables scientists to predict eclipses centuries in advance to the fraction of a second.

Sir Christopher Wren lies buried in London's St. Paul's Cathedral, the great church that this genius planned and built. On his tombstone is a simple Latin inscription that reads, "If you wish to see his monument, look around you." The psalmist invites us, if we want to see the glory of God, to look about us.

If we found a watch ticking on a desert island, we would know that somewhere there had to be a watchmaker to make an instrument of such complexity and design. The universe transcends the intelligent design and precision of the world's finest watch. Such a marvelous world must have a world-maker. Behind such an intelligent universe must be a Cosmic Intelligence, a Master Engineer.

If the limited knowledge available to the psalmist inspired him to such lofty eloquence, what would he have said if he had had the insights of modern astronomy? What if he had known that the earth, which seemed to him to be the center of things, was only a pygmy islet in a fathomless sea of intergalactic space? What if he had known that the light sparkling from a star left that star two million years ago to travel through fathomless space at its phantom speed of 186,000 miles per second?

Indeed, the skies proclaim the work of the Creator's hands in their beauty, their design, and their immensity. As Elizabeth Barrett Browning reminds us, "Earth's crammed with heaven." God speaks eloquently and unmistakably to us through his "World Book."

"Day after day they pour forth speech; night after night they display knowledge" (v. 2). The verb for "pour forth" means "to bubble up." Creation effervesces with its witness to the glory of God. How often we have been transfixed in awe before the glorious spectacle of a sunrise or the majesty of a star-bejeweled sky.

Nature's proclamation of God is universal. No one is left without a witness of God: "There is no speech or language where their voice is not heard. Their voice goes out into all the earth, their words to the end of the world" (v. 3). There are no language barriers, no national barriers. It has been said that the book of nature has three leaves – heaven, earth, and sea. All people everywhere may behold the majesty of the stars, the glory of a sunset, and the unending rhythm of ocean tides.

Elsewhere the psalmist exclaims: "All your salvation wonders are on display in your trophy room. Earth-Tamer, Ocean-Pourer, Mountain-Maker, Hill-Dresser . . . Dawn and dusk take turns calling, 'Come and worship.' Take a good look at God's wonders – they'll take your breath away" (65:5-6, 8; 66:5 in Eugene Peterson's paraphrase, *The Message*). William Barclay expressed it perceptively: "Approached with reverence, nature gives a glimpse into the interior of God's workshop." May we, with the psalmist, approach God's "World Book" with reverence and receive this "glimpse into the interior of God's workshop."

God, our Creator, we praise you for your radiant revelations in our world.

CHAPTER 12

The Word Book of God

PSALM 19, CONTINUED

> *The law of the LORD is perfect,*
> *reviving the soul.*
> (19:7)

THE PSALMIST HAS SPOKEN to us in lofty and eloquent terms of the heavens declaring the glory of God and the skies proclaiming the work of his hands. We cannot miss the signature of God on his handiwork – the beauty, orderliness, and immensity in the universe.

But something is missing! Nature can also be, as Tennyson puts it, "red in tooth and claw." The "World Book" presents God as a remote, vast, unapproachable, and, perhaps, vaguely disturbing cosmic power. This sheer otherworldliness of God does little to warm our hearts, comfort us, strengthen us, or direct us. God's communication through his "World Book," although eloquent and universal, is incomplete.

In the context of the incomprehensible reaches of time and space, it can seem preposterously arrogant to think that the God who created all this wonder is aware of our finite existence on this speck in space. And even more, that the Power that flung the galaxies and super clusters into space took upon himself our flesh on our tiny planet and bore abuse and death because he loved us!

The psalmist now provides an even more direct revelation of God. He leads us from what traditionally has been called *natural theology,* knowledge of God inferred from nature, to *revealed theology,* that truth about himself which God directly reveals to humankind. It is a transition from God's "World Book" to God's "Word Book." The psalmist now speaks to us in immortal words about the Word of God. He takes us from generalities to specifics, from the impersonal to the personal, from the amoral to the moral, from God's transcendence to his immanence.

More than three centuries ago, Blaise Pascal took up the task of defending the Christian faith to those who believed they could live without God. In his *Pensées,* he defines human superiority to nature: "It is not from space that I must seek my dignity, but from the government of my thought. By space, the universe encompasses and swallows me up like an atom; by thought I comprehend the world." The psalmist comprehends the world in the context of his faith in God.

God's Word Book, as defined by the psalmist, reveals the truth about God in the world around him. It gives the meaning of his own existence in what T. H. Huxley otherwise described, "an islet in the midst of an illimitable ocean of inexplicability."

How unfortunate that Huxley didn't take this psalm to heart and mind.

Astronaut John Glenn spoke of the indispensable role of the compass in flying:

> For the airplane to fulfill its mission, it must be given direction. We do this by reference to our compass. Now the force that runs the compass defies all our senses: you can't see, hear, touch, taste, or smell it. But we know it's there because we see the results. We can look at an instrument here in the cockpit, and we can see that our compass is pointing a certain direction. And we have faith that the force making that compass work will continue to make it work. All of us who fly have staked our lives thousands of times on the fact that this compass will give us the proper reading and will guide us where we should go.

God's Word is our unfailing compass. We can stake our lives on its dependability. It is, in the words of the psalmist, "trustworthy." With the anonymous eighteenth-century poet we affirm:

> *How firm a foundation, you saints of the Lord,*
> *Is laid for your faith in his excellent word!*
> *What more can he say than to you he hath said,*
> *To you who for refuge to Jesus have fled?*

Heavenly Father, help me ever to follow the unerring guidance of your Word.

CHAPTER 13

Radiant Revelations

PSALM 19, CONTINUED

> *The statutes of the* LORD *are trustworthy,*
> *making wise the simple.*
> (19:7b)

THE PSALMIST USES SIX different words to describe God's Word Book. The one with the broadest meaning is "law," representing God's teaching in all its fullness. Not only are there the cosmic laws that govern the orderliness and destiny of the celestial bodies of the universe, but there is also the moral law of God to govern the way and destiny of humankind. That law is found in the Word of God.

Law is meant to be kept, to be obeyed. We cannot break God's law, for it is immutable. Rather, when we transgress it, we break ourselves upon it.

"The law of the LORD is perfect" (v. 7a). God's revelations in his Word never fail. They are absolutely enduring and trustworthy in our world of decay and deception. Each synonym for God's Word reveals a facet of its revelation of God to human beings. Note the results when we read and heed it: "reviving the soul . . . making wise the simple . . . giving joy to the heart . . . giving light to the eyes" (vv. 7-8). The psalmist goes on to say, "By them is your servant warned; in keeping them there is great reward" (v. 11).

No wonder the psalmist said God's law is superior to that which is usually thought most priceless, gold. God's Word is more precious, more enduring. It is also sweeter, he said, than the sweetest thing he could name, "honey from the comb" (v. 10).

Is God's Word as precious and priceless as that to us? Do we share the psalmist's experience of God's Word "giving joy to the heart" (v. 8b)? Do we go to it as God's love letters that will ravish our hearts with joy? God's Word is his love letter to humankind. It is his priceless treasure to us, an anthology of divine thought, an index to eternal truths.

Samuel Logan Brengle offers a delightful analogy of how to enjoy the Word of God: "Read and study it as two young lovers read and study each other's letters. As soon as the mail brings a letter from his sweetheart, the young man grabs it and without waiting to see if there is not another letter for him runs off to a corner and reads and laughs and rejoices over it and almost devours it. He meditates on it day and night, and reads it over again and then again. He delights in that letter."

Other books are sources of information. The Bible was given for our transformation. There's a big difference between the books that people make and the Book that makes people. May we delight in the Word of God and meditate daily upon it. May it be for us a priceless treasure and a source of unending enrichment and joy.

Our psalmist next will lead us from contemplation on the World of God, and the Word of God, to the Way of God. God's progressive revelation to humankind leads us from the spinning galaxies and the recorded Word to his revelation in human hearts. Thus we come next to a personal application of God's revelation in the world and the Word.

God of creation, we thank and praise you for revealing yourself in such marvelous ways.

CHAPTER 14

Hidden Faults

PSALM 19, CONTINUED

> *Forgive my hidden faults.*
> (19:12)

THE PSALMIST HAS SHOWN how God reveals himself in his world and his Word. Now he portrays the ways of God in the more intimate workings of the human heart.

"Forgive my hidden faults" is the psalmist's prayer. From whom may our faults be hidden? Our faults may be hidden from others, and even from ourselves. We can become so adept at role playing that ultimately even we believe the role we play. Christian psychologist James Dolby points out that we may spend our lives learning to play the game of deception, concealing who we really are from our friends and loved ones. Because we have played the roles given us by our subculture, and because we are afraid to tell the truth about ourselves for fear of personal rejection and loss of love, we find the task of self-discovery very difficult and sometimes impossible. We have great difficulty in shedding the many layers of self-deception to eventually find our true self.

The prayer of the psalmist is profound, for it is desperately difficult and painful to have God show us those faults and sins of which we have been unaware. Albert Orsborn's lyric expresses that sentiment with the petition that there be "no surviving hidden sin."

What cure does the psalmist seek for such hidden faults? He prays that God's law, like the all-piercing, all-detecting rays of the sun, will search out all the deep hiding places of his soul and bring cleansing.

There potentially lurks in every life a Dr. Jekyll and Mr. Hyde complex. Some lives shelter two persons – the self we show to others and the real self; the person other people meet and the person unknown to them. "Putting on a front" for others and self-deception are slippery slopes that lead to disaster.

Edward Martin has identified this spiritual dichotomy in a writing titled, "My Name Is Legion":

> Within my earthly temple there's a crowd,
> There's one of us that's humble; one that's proud.
> There's one that's brokenhearted for his sins,
> And one who, unrepentant, sits and grins.
> There's one who loves his neighbor as himself,
> And one who cares for naught but fame and pelf.
> From much corroding care would I be free
> If once I could determine which is me.

The psalmist calls us to face ourselves honestly and to be cleansed of any "hidden faults." In his book *Mere Christianity*, C. S. Lewis writes on the cardinal sin of pride or self-deception:

> There is one vice of which no man in the world is free; which every one in the world loathes when he sees it in someone else; and of which hardly any people, except Christians, ever imagine that they are guilty themselves. I have heard people admit that they are bad-tempered, or that they cannot keep their heads about girls or drink, or even

that they are cowards. I do not think I have ever heard anyone who was not a Christian accuse himself of this vice. And at the same time I have seldom met anyone, who was not a Christian, who showed the slightest mercy to it in others. There is no fault which makes a man more unpopular, and no fault which we are more unconscious of in ourselves. And the more we have it ourselves, the more we dislike it in others. The vice I am talking of is Pride or Self-Conceit.

The Celestial Surgeon will lovingly remove from the believer the spiritual cancer of hidden faults. All is known to him, and he wills to make us healthy and holy. He provided a cure for us on Calvary.

Omniscient God, unto whom all hearts are open and from whom no secrets are hid, forgive and cleanse me of any "hidden sin."

CHAPTER 15

Words and Thoughts

PSALM 19, CONTINUED

> *May the words of my mouth and the meditation of my heart*
> *be pleasing in your sight,*
> *O LORD, my Rock and my Redeemer.*
> *(19:14)*

THIS SUBLIME PSALM CLOSES with one of the memorable short prayers of the Bible that has become a permanent part of Christian worship, both private and public. It is commonly used as a prayer before a sermon or at the conclusion of a time of worship or fellowship.

The prayer concerns two vital and related areas of life: that both our words and our thoughts will be pleasing to God. Our thoughts give birth to our words, so that when the source is pure then that which comes forth will be acceptable to God.

Socrates said, "Speak that I may see thee." We might expect him to say, "Speak so that I may hear thee." But the wise philosopher knew that our words reveal who we are. Every time we speak, the world "sees" us.

Not only our words but also our patterns of speech reveal us. Do we, for example, wait our turn to speak, or do we monopolize a conversation? Do we need to have the last word? Can we say, "I don't know"? Do we repeat ourselves badly? These and other verbal liabilities can reveal insensitivity or lack of modesty and grace. If Christ lives and reigns in us, others will see the evidence of him in our words as well as our actions.

Words are always moral, for they reveal the heart and soul of the one who utters them and they leave their impact on other lives. Our Lord has said that we shall be held accountable for every idle word. We are responsible for our words. As an anonymous poet reminds us:

> *A careless word may kindle strife;*
> *A cruel word may wreck a life;*
> *A bitter word may hate instill;*
> *A brutal word may smite and kill;*
> *A gracious word may smooth the way;*
> *A joyous word may light the day;*
> *A timely word may lessen stress;*
> *A loving word may heal and bless.*

Mother Teresa was the most revered woman in the world during her time. She saw the dying, the crippled, the unwanted, and the unloved as "Jesus in disguise." Her work among the dying on the streets of Calcutta became legendary. Awarded the Nobel Peace Prize, she was described as a "burning light in a dark time." What was the secret of her saintliness? Perhaps it is found in the response she gave one day to a reporter: "I am like a pencil in the hand of God. That is all. He does the writing. The pencil has only to be allowed to be used." We too can be "a pencil in the hand of God," with our words and deeds as instruments of his love and grace.

The psalmist addresses his prayer: "O LORD, my Rock and my Redeemer." That is the secret of the acceptable word in God's sight. Jesus Christ, our Lord and our Redeemer, abundantly answers this prayer of the believer through his grace and the work of his Spirit in our heart.

In an interview with General Eva Burrows when she was international leader of The Salvation Army, I asked, "For what would you want most to be remembered?" She replied, "My ambition, I would say simply and humbly, is just to please God. And I often laugh and say if ever somebody writes my epitaph, I would like just three words, 'She pleased God.'" May that be the highest ambition for each of us: that with the psalmist, we may live pleasing in his sight.

May the words of my mouth and the meditation of my heart be pleasing in your sight, O LORD, my Rock and my Redeemer.

CHAPTER 16

The Psalm of the Cross

PSALM 22

> *My God, my God, why have you forsaken me?*
> (22:1)

MARTIN LUTHER WOULD REMIND us that "The words of God are to be understood by the Word of God." Psalms 22 and 23 are prime examples of psalms suffused with the radiance of Christ.

Psalm 22 may well be called The Gospel According to David.

It is the psalm of the cross. It portrays Christ our Savior in his dying hour and gives his final words. It is a memorial of his infinite love for the world.

This is a psalm of sacred prophecy that finds its fulfillment in the death, resurrection, and exaltation of Jesus Christ. As Moses took off his shoes in the presence of God at the burning bush, so we must approach this holy of holies in the Psalter with reverence and devotion.

Written in the first person, it is none other than Jesus himself speaking prophetically from the pages of the Old Testament. It opens with the familiar fourth saying of Jesus from the cross: "My God, my God, why have you forsaken me?" In that moment, the Son of God experienced the forsakenness of God as a consequence of the world's sin which he bore. These words remind us that our salvation was purchased at a terrible cost.

"Why have you forsaken me?" That Jesus should in that dread moment on Calvary be forsaken by his heavenly Father is a mystery too profound for human comprehension. But one sacred truth is vouchsafed to us. God's Word tells us that it was our sins that brought Christ to the ignominy and suffering of Calvary. He loved us with such infinite love that he was willing to endure even that forsakenness by his heavenly Father, who had to turn his back on Calvary and enshroud it in darkness as his beloved Son became the sin-bearer for all humankind.

But in our Lord's dark night of the soul, he still lay hold on God: "My God, my God." That same affirmation will sustain us in our own dark night of the soul. In our moments of greatest extremity we can still have faith that God is for us and will ultimately work out his eternal purpose in our lives.

Sooner or later, we too may know what it is to seem forsaken by God. Writers of old time spoke of this experience as *Deus absconditus* – the God who is hidden. Saint John of the Cross named it "the dark night of the soul." In such times of desolation of the spirit, it seems that our prayers are but empty words, that God is hidden from us. These barren wastelands of the soul, of seeming abandonment by God, have come to the saints through the ages. We may live faithfully, yet find ourselves, in the words of George Buttrick, "beating on Heaven's door with bruised knuckles."

In such experiences, as Saint John of the Cross observes, two purifications occur. First, we are liberated from dependence upon exterior supports – success, approval, even the worship aids and symbols of our devotional lives. Second, we are liberated from dependence upon interior supports – pride, ambition, and self-deception. Our dependence upon these external and internal supports are shattered so that our soul can trust in God alone. Søren Kierkegaard reminds us, "God creates everything out of nothing – and everything which God is to use He first reduces to nothing."

During World War II, a nameless Jew hiding in Germany scratched on a basement wall the Star of David and the following lines:

I believe in the sun even when it is not shining.
I believe in love even when I do not feel it.
I believe in God even when He is silent.

Faith gives the victory, when all is darkness, still to know the assurance of God's love and presence. When circumstances or tragedy eclipse the sun from our sky, may we still be able to say, "My God, my God." Our lamp of faith is not extinguished by God's silence; but standing in the shadows, God will keep watch over his own.

"Yet you are enthroned as the Holy One" (v. 3) is the reassuring word in the night season of the soul. The darkness might momentarily obscure the presence of God, but not his holiness. The holiness of God stands forever sure amid life's raging storms and tempests. In darkness and sorrow, the heart should find comfort in this great attribute of God. His holiness assures his faithfulness and mercy. We may not always understand his ways; but because he is holy, we can trust in him.

Christ of Calvary, give me the faith that will hold on to God even in the darkest night of my soul.

CHAPTER 17

Calvary in Preview

PSALM 22, CONTINUED

> *My strength is dried up like a potsherd,*
> *and my tongue sticks to the roof of my mouth.*
> (22:15)

OUR LORD CONTINUES TO speak in the first person in the second part of this messianic psalm. In this moment on the cross, his words express ultimate condescension: "I am a worm" (v. 6).

Imagine these words spoken by the Sovereign of the universe! This extreme self-deprecation spoken by One whose eternal glory staggers the imagination!

This is the Son of God who "emptied himself," taking upon himself our frailty and finiteness. The Son of God became what we were so that he might make us what he is. The King of Glory went from riches to rags that we might go from rags to riches.

Men mocked and derided him before whom angels veil their faces and adore. The prophetic words of our Lord on the cross continue:

> All who see me mock me;
>   they hurl insults, shaking their heads:
> "He trusts in the LORD;
>   let the LORD rescue him."   (vv. 7-8)

We come upon a cryptic reference to the "bulls of Bashan" in verses 12-13. Bashan was a fertile country (Numbers 32:4) where cattle grew fat and strong (Deuteronomy 32:14) and were known for their fierceness. "Strong bulls of Bashan encircle me" refers to those in high positions of power and authority – the priests, elders, scribes, Pharisees, rulers, soldiers – who bellowed around the cross like the wild bulls of Bashan.

The terrible thirst of Christ on Calvary is prophesied in the words: "My strength is dried up like a potsherd, and my tongue sticks to the roof of my mouth" (v. 15). Nothing is so dry as a potsherd – a piece of broken pottery that has been baked dry in the fire. "My tongue sticks to the roof of my mouth." What is more torturous than unrelieved thirst?

"I thirst!" cried our Lord from the cross. Strange words coming from the lips of the One who made every river that flows through the valleys and every stream that cascades through the mountains! "I thirst." Strange words from One who made refreshing rains and life-giving moisture and treasures of the snow! "I thirst." Strange words from One who said, "Whoever drinks of the water I shall give him shall never thirst."

To what depths of suffering our Lord in his love went for us on Calvary! We cannot begin to fathom the divine humility and the infinite love of God represented in the ignominy and suffering of the cross. The Highest – stooping to the lowest! The Sovereign – becoming the Sufferer! We are constrained to confess with Isaac Watts:

> When I survey the wondrous cross
>   On which the Prince of Glory died,
> My richest gain I count but loss,
>   And pour contempt on all my pride.
>
> See, from his head, his hands, his feet,
>   Sorrow and love flow mingled down;
> Did e'er such love and sorrow meet,
>   Or thorns compose so rich a crown?
>
> Were the whole realm of nature mine,
>   That were a present far too small;
> Love so amazing, so divine,
>   Demands my soul, my life, my all.

Man of Sorrows, lead me from my self-absorption to self-surrender and self-denial.

CHAPTER 18

The Divine Paradox

PSALM 22, CONTINUED

> *They have pierced my hands and my feet.*
> (22:16)

"THEY HAVE PIERCED MY hands and my feet." These words are a remarkable prophecy of crucifixion. David, a Jew, knew only stoning to death as execution in 1000 B.C., yet he prophetically penned these words, which graphically describe a crucifixion.

Such a scene defies description. Calvary is too high, too deep, too fathomless to be captured or capsulized in words. God Incarnate on a felon's cross! The Son of God suffering the brutality and bestiality of human beings! He who created the universe and holds the stars in their courses, there a broken and bleeding figure, dying a criminal's death! What amazing love of God, that did all that for me and you!

A ship's passenger tells of a dark night when, while on deck, he suddenly heard a roaring, followed by a volcano bursting into flame. In those brief moments, he saw the fire that is forever burning in the heart of the mountain. As we look at Calvary, we see the love that is forever in the heart of God for each of us. With Charles Wesley we exclaim:

> *Amazing love! How can it be*
> *That thou, my God, shouldst die for me?*

We have lost sight of Calvary and the cross as they really were. Generations have hauled the cross from Golgotha's lonely and skull-shaped hill and placed it on towering steeples, in cloistered halls, or in colorful stained glass. But George MacLeod has given a trenchant description of Calvary:

> Jesus was not crucified in a cathedral between two candles, but on a cross between two thieves; on the town garbage-heap; at a crossroad so cosmopolitan that they had to write his title in Hebrew and in Latin and in Greek; at the kind of place where cynics talk smut, and thieves curse, and soldiers gamble. Because that is where He died. And that is what He died about. And that is what churchmen should be and what churchmen should be about.

The late Robert G. Lee often told of his first visit to the Holy Land. When he saw the Mount of Calvary, he said, so great was his excitement that he started to run and soon outdistanced his party in climbing the hill. When at last the guide caught up with him, he asked, "Sir, have you been here before?" For a moment there was silence. Then, in whispered awe, Dr. Lee replied, "Yes, I was here, nearly two thousand years ago."

Indeed, we were all at Calvary nearly two thousand years ago. We were there under the sentence of death in the divine judgment upon sin. But we were also there in the amazing grace of God, as Christ took that condemnation upon himself, that we might know the liberty of his salvation.

The writer of Hebrews invokes our contemplation of both our Lord's suffering and his triumph on Calvary: "Let us fix our eyes on Jesus, the author and perfecter of our faith, who for the joy set before him endured the cross, scorning its shame, and sat down at the right hand of the throne of God" (Hebrews 12:2). Our contemplation of the unimaginable suffering of the Son of God upon the cross, and his mighty triumph over its evil, surpasses our understanding but wins our hearts.

Lord, make Calvary real and transforming to me.

CHAPTER 19

History's Greatest Gamble

PSALM 22, CONTINUED

> *They divide my garments among them*
> *and cast lots for my clothing.*
> (22:18)

THE REMARKABLE PROPHECY OF this psalm continues with reference to the gambling for the clothing of our Lord at Calvary. One of the perquisites of the four soldiers carrying out the crucifixion was the clothes of the victim. Jesus, as was the custom among Jews, would have had five articles of apparel. Four articles had been divided, and only the seamless robe was left for which they diced. Soldiers gambling at the foot of the cross fulfilled this precise prophecy.

But Christ was also a gambler on Calvary! His were the highest stakes of history. It was history's greatest gamble – a divine life poured out in crude and cruel execution to win the salvation of the world. Countless redeemed and radiant lives have testified that Christ won that day.

G. Studdert-Kennedy has expressed it in unforgettable words:

And sitting down, they watched him there,
The soldiers did;
There, while they played with dice,
He made his sacrifice,
And died upon the cross to rid
God's world of sin.
He was a gambler, too, my Christ,
He took his life and threw
It for a world redeemed.
And ere his agony was done,
Before the westering sun went down,
Crowning that day with crimson crown,
He knew that He had won.

In A.D. 33, the cross was a symbol of shame. But since then, the world has gloried in it, carving it in many forms of beauty. It has been emblazoned on the flags of nations and engraved on the scepters and diadems of kings. The cross, planted on Golgotha as a dry, dead tree, struck its roots deep down into the heart of the world, blossomed, and sent its branches outward, till today nations rest beneath its shadow and are nurtured by its fruits.

"The cross," writes John R. W. Stott in *The Cross of Christ,* "transforms everything. The cross enforces three truths about ourselves, about God and about Jesus Christ. First, our sin must be extremely horrible. Nothing reveals the gravity of sin like the cross. Second, God's love must be wonderful beyond comprehension. Third, Christ's salvation must be a free gift."

The cross is indeed God's supreme revelation of love for the world. In their devotion to the One who suffered upon it, cross bearers have been inspired to sing the words of George Bennard:

> On a hill far away stood an old rugged cross,
>   The emblem of suffering and shame,
> And I love that old cross where the dearest and best
>   For a world of lost sinners was slain.
>   So I'll cherish the old rugged cross
>   Till my trophies at last I lay down;
>   I will cling to the old rugged cross
>   And exchange it some day for a crown.

Eternal Love, on the cross beams I see the gravity of my sin and the marvelous grace of my Savior.

CHAPTER 20

Great Expectations

PSALM 22, CONTINUED

> They will proclaim his righteousness
> to a people yet unborn –
> for he has done it.
>
> (22:31)

THERE IS A MARKED transition starting with the twenty-second verse of this psalm. It progresses from minor to major key. The raging tempest becomes a comforting calm. Our Savior turns his eyes from his suffering to the glory that follows. He anticipates the blessings of his passion and exaltation and breaks forth into exulting predictions and praise:

> I will declare your name to my brothers;
> in the congregation I will praise you. . . .
> All the ends of the earth
> will remember and turn to the LORD,
> and all the families of the nations
> will bow down before him,
> for dominion belongs to the LORD
> and he rules over the nations.
>
> (vv. 22, 27-28)

This sacred psalm does not end with execution but with the exaltation of our Lord. It leads us from his cross to his

crown as all nations pay him homage and he is ascribed universal dominion.

The psalm calls us to devotion and dedication to Jesus
Christ as Savior and Sovereign of our life. In deepest gratitude
to such an amazing love, we kneel in humble adoration and acknowledge his undisputed sovereignty. Let the cross speak its
message to us in the poem of William L. Stidger:

I am the cross of Christ.
I bore his body there
On Calvary's lonely hill.
Till then I was a humble tree
That grew beside a tiny rill;
I think till then
I was a thing despised of men!

I am the cross of Christ!
I felt his limbs along
My common, broken bark;
I saw his utter loneliness,
The lightning and the dark;
And up till then
I thought He was as other men.

I am the cross of Christ!
On my form they used to crucify
The outcasts of the earth;
But on the lonely hill that day
My kind received, in blood, new birth,
And ever till this day
A weary world bows at my feet to pray!

I am the cross of Christ.
They say I tower "o'er the wrecks
Of time." I only know
That once, a humble tree,
This was not so. But this
I know – since then
I have become a symbol for the hopes of men.

Victorious Lord, may your cross ever be my badge of triumph.

CHAPTER 21

The Good Shepherd

PSALM 23

> The LORD *is my shepherd.*
> (23:1)

PSALM 23 IS THE brightest jewel of the Psalms. For nearly three thousand years it has been among the best-known and best-loved texts of the Bible. C. H. Spurgeon writes of this psalm: "Its piety and its poetry are equal. Its sweetness and its spirituality are unsurpassed." Henry Ward Beecher, eloquent preacher of yesteryear, eulogized: "It has filled the whole world with melodious joy. It has charmed more griefs to rest than all the philosophy of the world. Nor is its work done. It will go on singing to your children, and to their children, through all the generations of time; nor will it fold its wings till the last pilgrim is safe, and time ended; and then it shall fly back to the bosom of God, whence it issued, and sound on, mingled with all those sounds of celestial joy which make heaven musical forever."

But it is only after Psalm 22, where we meet Christ as Savior, that we can come to Psalm 23 and know him as Shepherd. The Apostle Paul declared, "For I delivered to you first of all that which I also received: that Christ died for our sins" (1 Cor. 15:3, NKJV). "First of all" – the fact of Christ's sacrifice takes first rank and has priority and precedence over all other proclamations. We must go by the blood-sprinkled path of Calvary to enter the quiet green pastures of the Shepherd's care. It is only because of Christ's agonizing cry on the cross in Psalm 22, "My God, my God, why have you forsaken me?" that we are able to say, "The LORD is my shepherd" in Psalm 23.

This psalm speaks prophetically of the One who would become the Good Shepherd, laying down his life for his sheep. Jesus applied this metaphor to himself in his sublime statement, "I am the good shepherd" (John 10:11). He likened himself to the shepherd who had one hundred sheep, with ninety-nine safe in the fold and one that was lost. The shepherd went into the wilderness and sought and found the lost sheep, rejoicing upon his return (Luke 15:1-7). Psalm 23 portrays the Good Shepherd who sought and found us when we were lost, resulting in joy for all who have wandered astray.

We need to transpose the truths and teachings in the Psalms from their rural imagery to our day of space exploration and urban lifestyle. We know so little about sheep and shepherds. The pastoral setting and imagery of this psalm require some transposition. Eugene Peterson has helped us in that direction with his modern paraphrase of the Psalms, putting them in easy-to-read modern language, while retaining the rhythm, idioms, and earthy flavor of the original Hebrew; his renderings of familiar passages are just as fresh, relevant, and surprising as the originals were for their first readers centuries ago. For example, the New International Version renders verse 5: "You anoint my head with oil; my cup overflows." Peterson's paraphrase reads: "You revive my drooping head; my cup brims with blessing." The Scripture, written in the language of the people of its day, often brings fresh insight when contemporized in the words and images of our own time.

At the same time, the venerable phrasing and imagery of this psalm remain timely and timeless. "The LORD is my shepherd." Let us look more closely at this familiar statement.

The Lord – he who is the suffering Savior of Psalm 22, he who is the Lord of creation – would be our Shepherd. I, a mere mortal, become a cherished object of divine care. The common clay of my humanity can be linked with divine destiny in Christ.

My Shepherd – the psalmist doesn't refer to the Lord as the Shepherd of all the world; rather, he is confident in the Lord's personal relationship and care as his very own Shepherd. "The sweetest word of the whole psalm is that monosyllable *my*," writes Spurgeon.

Shepherd – it is hardly a romantic vocation. Rather it is fatiguing, with long hours and isolation. It requires dealing with creatures prone to stray, being assaulted by storms, fighting wild beasts and robbers. The Lord takes on that role for us. He does not dwell in isolated splendor in his celestial sanctuary. As our Shepherd, he came to dwell among us and laid down his life for us. He now walks with us on our human pathway, guiding us in our helplessness and need as we make our pilgrimage to the eternal home he is preparing for us.

The story is told of two men who once repeated the Twenty-third Psalm to a large audience. One was a polished orator, who repeated the psalm in an eloquent fashion. When he finished, the audience gave a prolonged applause. Then the other man, somewhat older, repeated the same words. But when he finished, no sound at all came from the audience. Instead, the people were hushed, as though in a spirit of prayer. Then the polished orator stood up and said, "Friends, I wish to offer an explanation of what has happened here tonight. You gave to me your applause, but when my friend had finished, you remained reverently silent. The difference is, I know the Psalm, but he knows the Shepherd."

Sovereign God, thank you for your infinite love that led you to become my Savior and Shepherd.

CHAPTER 22

The Lord's Providence

PSALM 23, CONTINUED

> *I shall not want.*
> (23:1b, NKJV)

THE PSALMIST AFFIRMS, "I shall not want." This is not a reference to his material but to his spiritual needs. "No good thing does he withhold from those whose walk is blameless" – this is the Lord's promise to his people (Psalm 84:11). A "good thing" is that which ennobles and enriches the soul.

"He makes me lie down in green pastures" (v. 2a) speaks of the nurture and sustenance our divine Shepherd gives for the soul. We have an innate hunger and thirst for God. Jesus said, "Blessed are those who hunger and thirst for righteousness" (Matthew 5:6). Our souls are nourished by the truths of his Word, and our spirits are refreshed by prayer.

"He leads me beside the still waters" (v. 2b, NKJV) describes the Shepherd's provision for peace. Henry David Thoreau gave his diagnosis of his generation when he wrote: "The mass of men lead lives of quiet desperation." Such desperation seems all the more common in our era as people are caught up in the syndrome of busyness, living life in the fast lane. As the Chinese proverb reminds us, man cannot see himself in running water. We need those quiet pools for reflection – to discover who we really are – and for renewal – to actualize our potential.

In the midst of our world's chaos and confusion, our Good Shepherd will lead us in the path of inner peace.

The prophet Jeremiah gives us a compelling metaphor for broken lives and shattered dreams: "My people have . . . forsaken me, the spring of living water, and have dug their own cisterns, broken cisterns that cannot hold water" (Jeremiah 2:13). Many today try to quench the thirst of their parched lives with education, travel, careers, hobbies, sexual adventure. They drink from the broken cisterns of drugs or materialism and find that the waters fail. The Good Shepherd alone can lead us beside the still waters that satisfy and quench the deepest thirsts of life.

We note that refreshment beside the still waters and green pastures precedes the severest part of the journey yet to come. It is not enough to call upon God only when trouble strikes. Reserves of spiritual energy must be secured for the difficult days ahead when the enemies of our soul will make their fierce attack and we must go through the dark valley that awaits.

The writer of the fourth Gospel tells us that the Good Shepherd "goes on ahead of them" (John 10:4). He does not drive his sheep but leads them. Christ has traveled the way before us. He has journeyed through life's thorn-grown wilderness and its deep chasms. He knows life's testings and perils. He leads his sheep "beside the still waters," for a rushing current might sweep the flock away to destruction or mask the sound of an approaching enemy.

But the Good Shepherd does not lead us continually in pastures green or by still waters. He is also with us amid the tempests and storms and down in the deep valleys of life. We have his assurance that his presence will always be there beside us. Christians may sing with confidence the words of Joseph

Gilmore, which, though penned almost a century ago, still ring true:

> *He leadeth me! O blessed thought!*
> *O words with heavenly comfort fraught!*
> *Whate'er I do, where'er I be,*
> *Still 'tis God's hand that leadeth me.*
>
> *Sometimes 'mid scenes of deepest gloom,*
> *Sometimes where Eden's bowers bloom,*
> *By waters still, o'er troubled sea,*
> *Still 'tis his hand that leadeth me.*
>
> *Lord, I would clasp thy hand in mine,*
> *Nor ever murmur or repine,*
> *Content, whatever lot I see,*
> *Since 'tis my God that leadeth me.*
>
> *And when my task on earth is done,*
> *When by thy grace the victory's won,*
> *E'en death's cold wave I will not flee,*
> *Since God through Jordan leadeth me.*

Shepherd, lead me to fresh, sweet springs of soul sustenance and renewal.

CHAPTER 23

The Lord's Provision

PSALM 23, CONTINUED

> *He restores my soul.*
> (23:3a)

"THE GREAT MALADY OF the twentieth century, implicated in all of our troubles and affecting us individually and socially, is loss of soul." With this seminal diagnosis, Thomas Moore launched his 1994 bestseller, *Care of the Soul*. He observes further: "When soul is neglected, it doesn't just go away; it appears symptomatically in obsessions, addictions, violence, and loss of meaning. Soul is the font of who we are. It has to do with depth, value, relatedness, heart, and personal substance."

"He restores my soul" is the assurance of the Shepherd's provision for renewal. How often we have need for the renewal of soul. We experience constant erosion of our spiritual resources and need the Lord's replenishment and restoration. The restoring of our souls relates to many needs of life. When we are sorrowful, he comforts; when we are sinful, he forgives; when we are weak, he strengthens; when we are perplexed, he guides; when we fail, he lifts us up. When our energies were spent and our souls heavily burdened, we came to the Good Shepherd and he restored our souls. Drooping powers were quickened, burdens relieved, and our souls refreshed and set at peace. Our Good Shepherd provides the ultimate care and cure for the soul, without which it will be lost.

Alan Redpath, when he was pastor of the Moody Church in Chicago, had this motto hanging on the wall of his study: "Beware of the barrenness of a busy life." Busyness rapes relationships, feeds the ego but starves the inner person, fills a calendar but fractures a family. Today we all too easily find that "the world is too much with us" (Wordsworth). We become caught up in a tornado of activity, a torrent of voices, a tumult of noise. With Augustine we confess, "I lost myself among a multiplicity of things." We need to stop, to pause beside the Lord's green pastures and quiet waters, to take in, to be restored and renewed.

"He leads me in the paths of righteousness" (v. 3, NKJV) is his promise of guidance. Sheep are notoriously wayward, prone to get lost if left alone. We confess the sheepishness of our own nature, as Isaiah reminds us: "We all, like sheep, have gone astray, each of us has turned to his own way" (Isaiah 53:6). We have been prone to wander, to go foolishly astray. The sheep is a dependent creature, always needing some help, lest it become lost and in danger. This psalm gives the blessed assurance that we have a Shepherd who will guide us away from the pitfalls and perils and lead us safe in the path of righteousness.

We need to turn the leadership of our life over to Christ, who is our Good Shepherd. We tend to go our own way and need to be liberated from self-pleasing so that we live simply for God. The Lord will shepherd us only if we hear and heed his voice and follow where he leads.

An anonymous author penned a timeless truth of the Lord's leading and presence:

In 'pastures green'? Not always; sometimes He
Who knoweth best, in kindness leadeth me
In weary ways, where heavy shadows be.

And by 'still waters'? No, not always so;
Oft times the heavy tempests round me blow,
And o'er my soul the waves and billows go.

But when the storm beats loudest, and I cry
Aloud for help, the Master standeth by,
And whispers to my soul, "Lo, it is I."

So, where He leads me, I can safely go,
And in the blest hereafter I shall know,
Why, in his wisdom He hath led me so.

Lord, I am so prone to stray. Take my hand and lead me, lest I fail and
fall.

CHAPTER 24

The Lord's Presence

PSALM 23, CONTINUED

> *Even though I walk*
> *through the valley of the shadow of death,*
> *I will fear no evil.*
> (23:4)

THE SHEPHERD'S PRESENCE IS with us, not only all through life, but even when we come to its termination.

The word "walk" indicates the steady advance of a soul. Death is not the end, but a continued progress in the plan of God. The believer approaches the end of life, not flurried or frantic, but calm and composed. There is no need for alarm, because we are in the company of the Good Shepherd. Fear is eclipsed by his presence.

We do not stay in death, but walk *through* its valley. Death is but a thoroughfare to the new, bright, shining world to which the Chief Shepherd leads us. William Barclay writes: "The end of life is God. The last step of life is the step which leads into the presence of God."

A little girl whose path from school led through a graveyard was asked if she were afraid. "No," she answered, "I just cross it to reach home." This psalm eloquently declares that death is not a dead end but a pathway to the house of the Lord.

The psalmist likens death to a valley. Every mountain has its valley. The mountainsides may be scarred by deep ravines, gulches, or gullies, but valleys need not be forbidding places. They are most often well-watered with springs, streams, and rivers, with rich feed and forage along the route. As souls come to this valley in their pilgrimage, they will find even there provision to sustain them, enabling them to pass through.

Malcolm Muggeridge wrote of "being in love with death." Some would accuse him of morbidity. But Muggeridge explained the need to see the limitations of this life, and he longed to break free of them "because death is life's fulfillment." He likened humans to a caterpillar who must shuffle off a worn chrysalis in order to fly away.

This radiant psalm reminds us that death is not substance, but shadow. It is not the valley of death, but the valley of the *shadow* of death. Where there is a shadow, there must be light. Let us look beyond the shadow of death to the Light of the World.

When we come to this consummating experience of our lives, may our confident testimony ring out with the psalmist: "I will fear no evil, for you are with me" (v. 4). The sense of Christ's presence is real to the Christian, in life, at death, and beyond the grave. "For you are with me" is the eternal assurance of the believer.

The Apostle John wrote: "We know that we have passed from death to life" (1 John 3:14). This statement reverses the world's order of things, which is to pass from life to death. But the believer, as a daughter or a son of the Resurrection, passes from death to life, from mortality to immortality, from the temporal to the eternal, to dwell in God's house forevermore.

The great preacher Spurgeon told of an epitaph he once spied in an obscure country cemetery in England. The headstone was small and of inexpensive material, and on it were chiseled just two words. On top, "Freddy!" as if someone had called a boy's name. Underneath, as if the boy had answered, just one word, "Yes." The Christ who walks with us on the earthly road is the Christ who will meet us at our Father's eternal home. The valley of the shadow of death becomes a thoroughfare to God and heaven.

Eternal Christ, deliver me from any fear of death by your presence and power.

CHAPTER 25

The Lord's Protection

PSALM 23, CONTINUED

> *Your rod and your staff, they comfort me.*
> (23:4b)

THIS PEARL OF THE Psalms approaches its climax with a beautiful description of the Good Shepherd's guardian care of us. The shepherd's rod, a stout piece of wood, helped him to protect the sheep and himself. With it he would drive off predators such as lions, jackals, wolves, or wild dogs.

The path of life on which we travel has its perils along the way. Many enemies of our soul would likewise destroy us. We need our Shepherd's protection, his guardian care all along our pilgrim pathway. With the poet Albert Orsborn, we would pray for the Shepherd's guidance and protection amid life's rugged terrain:

> Unto thee will I cry,
> Shepherd, hear my prayer!
> Poor and needy am I,
> Shepherd, hear my prayer!
> Deep is calling unto deep,
> Rugged are the heights and steep;
> Guide my steps and keep;
> Hear, O hear my prayer!

With his rod, the shepherd also disciplined the sheep for their own good and safety. Sometimes we – like David, the author of this psalm – need the Lord's chastening to remain true and faithful in following him.

The staff, a long slender stick with a crook at one end, is that which most readily identifies the shepherd. In the Christian church it has become a symbol of pastoral and ecclesiastical leadership. With it the shepherd reaches out and puts the crook around the neck of the sheep, drawing it close for examination and care. He uses the staff to guide his sheep where they will be safe and nourished. Or, if a sheep slips down a steep cliff, he can reach down with his staff and lift the sheep to safety.

Philip Keller, writing out of shepherd experience and with biblical insight in his book *A Shepherd Looks at Psalm 23*, explains the value of the shepherd's staff:

Another common occurrence was to find sheep stuck fast in labyrinths of wild roses or brambles where they had pushed in to find a few stray mouthfuls of green grass. Soon the thorns were so hooked in their wool they could not possibly pull free, tug as they might. Only the use of the staff could free them from their entanglement. Likewise with us. Many of our jams and impasses are of our own making. In stubborn, self-willed, self-assertion we keep intruding into situations where we cannot extricate ourselves. Then in compassion and care our Shepherd comes to us. He draws near and in tenderness lifts us by his Spirit out of the difficulty and dilemma. What patience God has with us!

Our Good Shepherd protects us with his rod, and sometimes he also chastens us for our good. With his staff, he draws us near to himself. He guides us and rescues us. When we follow him, we are ever under his guardian care.

May we know these blessings of the Good Shepherd – his providence, his provision, his presence, his protection, and (as we next shall consider) his promise.

Good Shepherd, I bow in awe and adoration before the ample provision you have made for me.

CHAPTER 26

The Lord's Promise

PSALM 23, CONTINUED

> *I will dwell in the house of the* LORD *forever.*
> (23:6)

THE GOOD SHEPHERD PREPARES "a table before me" (v. 5a). He makes provision for my every need. The Apostle Paul further affirms this truth for us: "My God shall supply all your need according to His riches in glory by Christ Jesus" (Philippians 4:19, NKJV). God's table does not supply all our wishes, but rather the deep needs of our soul.

"You anoint my head with oil" (v. 5c). The strong, tender hands of the shepherd rubbed oil into the head of the sheep to relieve aggravations, infestation, irritations, wounds. Our Good Shepherd, with the anointing of his Spirit, relieves the irritations of life and cleanses and heals the festerings of the soul.

"My cup overflows" (v. 5d). He provides not only abundance, but redundance. His blessings are so ample that they spill over to other lives.

"Surely goodness and love will follow me all the days of my life" (v. 6a). Expositors point out that shepherds usually have at least two dogs as companions and invaluable helpers. They sometimes suggest that the shepherd's two dogs, with their special care and guarding of the sheep, are named "goodness" and "mercy." "Surely" speaks of the psalmist's confidence, and "follow me all the days of my life" speaks of the constancy of the Lord's goodness and mercy.

The Good Shepherd of this magnificent psalm now leads us to our final destination: "I will dwell in the house of the LORD forever" (v. 6b). What a precious promise – both for our loved ones who have gone from this life and for our own eternity.

While touring the St. Calixtus Catacombs in Rome, I was captivated by the third-century paintings on the underground rock wall. They bore a revealing testimony to the life and thought of the early church. Among those ancient and rare paintings was one of Christ as the Good Shepherd, carrying a sheep over his shoulder. This concept of Christ as the Good Shepherd has been one of the most endearing portraits of our Lord through the centuries. It graces the walls of many Christian homes and churches as well as the imagination of devout believers.

The Scottish Psalter provides this paraphrase of Psalm 23, wedded to a stately tune in which modern singers may express the assurance of this sublime psalm:

The Lord's my Shepherd, I'll not want;
He makes me down to lie
In pastures green, He leadeth me
The quiet waters by.

My soul He doth restore again,
And me to walk doth make
Within the paths of righteousness,
E'en for his own name's sake.

Yea, though I walk in death's dark vale,
Yet will I fear no ill,

For thou art with me, and thy rod
And staff me comfort still.

My table thou hast furnished
In presence of my foes;
My head thou dost with oil anoint,
And my cup overflows.

Goodness and mercy all my life
Shall surely follow me;
And in God's house for evermore
My dwelling place shall be.

Good Shepherd, lead me through life's valley and maze to my Father's house.

CHAPTER 27

From the Cross to the Crown

PSALM 24

> The earth is the LORD's.
> (24:1)

A JEWEL SHINES MOST brightly when viewed in the best setting. The brightest gem of the Psalter, Psalm 23, shines all the brighter when seen in the context of the psalms that immediately precede and follow it. On one side of its valleys and green pastures is Mt. Calvary of Psalm 22, and on the other is Mt. Zion in Psalm 24.

The psalmist leads us from the psalm of the Savior's cross to the psalm of the Shepherd's crook, and now to the psalm of the Sovereign's crown. In Psalm 22 we see our Lord who saves us, in Psalm 23 our Lord who shepherds us, and in Psalm 24 our Lord who reigns over us and is coming again for us. This trilogy portrays the past, present, and future; our Lord dying, living, and reigning; his grace, guidance, and glory.

C. H. Spurgeon describes how the Spirit enabled the psalmist to touch the mournful string of his harp in Psalm 22, to pour forth gentle notes of peace in Psalm 23, and here, in Psalm 24, to utter majestic and triumphant strains. So too, under the inspiration of the Holy Spirit, we can pour forth our songs of sorrow, peace, and triumph.

Psalm 24 is interpreted by many as prophetic of the ascension and ultimate sovereignty of Jesus Christ. Its portrayal of Christ as the "King of glory" strikes an eternal chord of truth. We need a full-orbed theology of Christ that takes us both before and beyond his earthly life. John, in his beatific vision on the Isle of Patmos, envisioned him as "Lord of lords and King of kings" (Revelation 17:14). Christ rules with absolute and unchallenged supremacy over all who have had brief earthly kingdoms and dynasties. The coming of Christ in glory is the ultimate goal of all history and the grand expectation of all believers.

"The earth is the LORD's." The imagination staggers at the thought of his proprietorship over, not merely planet earth, but the cosmos. The infinite depths of the universe are his habitation. The title "Lord" is used of Christ by the Apostle Paul more than two hundred times, denoting his ownership, authority, and deity. There is a wholeness about the life of Christ that needs to be perceived. The tapestry of his life must be looked on as a whole to see its design and beauty. We need to know Christ, not only as Savior, but also as Lord whose dominion includes all things, in heaven and on earth.

Even those figures of history who did not accept the claims of Christ as Savior were impressed with his transcendent greatness and glory. Napoleon, during his almost twenty years of imprisoned exile on the island of Elba, spent many of his days studying the life and leadership of Jesus Christ. He recorded: "I know men; and I tell you that Jesus Christ is not a man. There is between Christianity and whatever other religions the distance of infinity. Between Christ and whoever else in the world there is no possible term of comparison. I tell you, all these [the heroes of antiquity] were men and I am a man, but not one is like him; Jesus Christ was more than man."

Indeed, Christ reigns in unapproachable glory, and with the psalmist we in reverence acknowledge: "The earth is the LORD's, and everything in it, the world, and all who live in it!"

The psalmist here presents a lofty conception of Christ, of whom, in the words of Thomas Kelly, we may sing:

The head that once was crowned with thorns
  Is crowned with glory now;
A royal diadem adorns
  The mighty Victor's brow.

The highest place that Heaven affords
  Is his, is his by right,

The King of kings and Lord of lords
　And Heaven's eternal light.

Lord Jesus, I acknowledge you as my Savior, my Shepherd, and my Sovereign.

CHAPTER 28

Environmental Sins and Stewardship

PSALM 24, CONTINUED

> *The earth is the LORD's, and everything in it,*
> *the world, and all who live in it.*
> (24:1)

HUMAN BEINGS HAVE "CONQUERED" the earth by military might and disposed of it in petty states and kingdoms. But the earth does not belong to humankind. "The earth is the LORD's" declares the psalmist. Humankind is but a tenant, a leaseholder, with the most precarious tenure. God is the owner; all of planet earth and the cosmos is under his sovereignty.

"Everything in it" speaks of the marvels and mysteries of the world God has given for our sustenance and enjoyment. Theologian John Calvin writes of this phrase: "Under the word 'fullness' all the riches with which the earth is adorned are comprehended."

Human "inventions" are merely discoveries of what God has bestowed in the earth. Electricity was hidden in the earth long before people discovered it and learned to use it. So it was with oil, chloroform, penicillin, and so many other benefits God implanted in the earth for human good. Science has been a treasure hunt, with scientists as the hunters and God as the originator of the treasure.

Divine proprietorship of the earth requires human stewardship. Conservation of the earth's beauty, resources, and purity becomes a moral obligation. With knowledge of how fragile is our ecosystem and awareness that the environment is reeling from abuse and neglect, Christians today should be in the vanguard of those actively concerned about the despoliation of the earth. From the stratosphere to the seven seas, from global warming to ocean fouling, virtually every habitat and natural resource is threatened. Let us not allow the good and beautiful earth the Lord has given us to be polluted and its life-sustaining resources destroyed by acid rain, nuclear fallout, toxic wastes, and other environmental sins for which the great Landowner and True Proprietor will hold his tenants accountable.

The psalmist calls us to a theocentric or God-centered perception of our world as he reminds us: "The earth is the LORD's, and everything in it." Therefore it must have our most responsible care. Let us not march to the drumbeat of political expediency or unbridled consumerism that exploits the marvelous environment given us by the Creator. As someone once said, "It is time we steered by the stars and not by the light of each passing ship."

"The world, and all who live in it" makes divine proprietorship highly personal. Whatever befalls the earth also befalls the children of the earth. God is the proprietor not only of the earth, but also of my life. People belong to their Creator as much as the physical realm does. We are a part of God's marvelous world, the crown of his creation.

Help us, Lord, to be faithful stewards of the rich bounty of the earth you have given us.

CHAPTER 29

Clean Hands and a Pure Heart

PSALM 24, CONTINUED

> *Who may ascend the hill of the LORD?*
> *Who may stand in his holy place?*
> *He who has clean hands and a pure heart.*
> (24:3-4)

AS WE CONTINUE OUR meditation on what has been called "the Ascension Psalm," a question is posed that is always in season for the soul:

> *Who may ascend the hill of the LORD?*
> *Who may stand in his holy place?*

The highest ambition of our soul should be to reach the holy place of God's presence, to enjoy constant fellowship with him. But who can enjoy such unspeakable blessedness? Who can ascend to such heights? Who can know the secret of his presence? Is such an Everest of attainment possible for finite, frail, and faltering human beings like us?

The psalmist does not leave us without an answer: "He who has clean hands and a pure heart, who does not lift up his soul to an idol or swear by what is false" (v. 4).

Have we been restless, unsatisfied by the things of the world? Have we been longing for the fuller, richer life that God has for us? Have we had visions of heights for our feet, yet untrod; songs of rejoicing and victory fashioned for our lips, yet unsung; closeness of communion with the Lord, yet unrealized? This psalm invites us to those heights, to the very presence of God.

But the sacred privilege carries its responsibilities. Our hands, the outward practical life, must be clean. Our hearts, the inward life with its motivations and innermost thoughts, must be pure. The blessing is bestowed upon the one who has not failed and grieved God with ill-kept vows.

Such communion with God is attained by an upward path, for we "ascend" this height of holy and divine fellowship. This pilgrimage of the soul has its required disciplines, renunciations, and dedications. We must remove everything that stands in the way of our union with God. The work of the cleansing of our soul will be a lifetime process. Our perfection consists of struggling against our imperfection.

One day an eagle was mortally wounded by a rifle shot. He slowly turned his head and gave one more longing look at the sky that had been his domain. He had often swept those starry spaces with his majestic wings. The beautiful sky was the home of his heart. A thousand times he had enjoyed there his splendid strength. In its faraway heights he had raced with the winds. And now, far from home, the eagle lay dying. All because once he forgot and flew too low.

Such is the epitaph of many a life. Instead of living on the heights of holiness, they suffer defeat and spiritual death amid the spiritual lowlands of the moral pollution and enticements of the world.

Our petition is well framed in William Pennick's song:

There is a holy hill of God,
*   Its heights by faith I see;*
Now to ascend my soul aspires
*   To leave earth's vanity.*

Lord, cleanse my hands and cleanse my heart,
*   All selfish aims I flee;*
My faith reward, thy love impart
*   And let me dwell with thee.*

The person with clean hands, pure heart, and faithful vows "will receive blessing from the LORD and vindication from God his Savior" (v. 5). By full surrender and faith, we may appropriate the blessing of clean hands and a pure heart and fellowship with the Lord of the universe.

Crystal Christ, impart to me your gift of clean hands and a pure heart that I may more worthily love and serve you.

CHAPTER 30

The King of Glory

PSALM 24, CONTINUED

> *Who is this King of glory?*
> *The LORD strong and mighty,*
> *the LORD mighty in battle.*
> (24:8)

IN THE TWICE-REPEATED question and answer of the final four verses of Psalm 24, we have no less than the eternal drama of the human soul:

> *Lift up your heads, O you gates;*
> *be lifted up, you ancient doors,*
> *that the King of glory may come in.*
> *Who is this King of glory?*
> *The LORD strong and mighty,*
> *The LORD mighty in battle.*   (vv. 7-10)

What are these gates that need to be opened? What are the barriers that would prevent the entrance of the King of glory?

Job, with a haunting question, named one gate that mortals cannot open themselves: "Have the gates of death been opened unto you?" (Job 38:17, KJV). And there is the gate of entrenched evil in the world, the gate of pain and of sorrow. But above all there is the gate of the human heart that may remain bolted and barred against the Lord's entrance. But the King of glory himself condescends, comes to the very door of our hearts, and invites us to open and let him in.

"Who is this King of glory?" It is a question worthy of our most serious thought. The full choir must join in the antiphonal response: "The LORD strong and mighty, the LORD mighty in battle." We know him by the battles he has fought and won for us, his victories over sin, death, and hell.

Pascal wrote of the Great Wager of life. He stated that either God exists or he does not. You must take sides on the issue. You must bet. If you wager for God and he does not exist, you will lose only a finite value of dubious quality, after all; at the most you will risk leading a life based on an error, but one that is on the whole noble and advantageous. But if you wager against God and God exists, you will lose all the joy of eternal life with him.

One of the great masterpieces of Christian art is Holman Hunt's painting *The Light of the World.* It is a devotional experience to look upon this noble work of art in St. Paul's Cathedral in London. In the painting, the artist visualized the text: "Here I am! I stand at the door and knock. If anyone hears my voice and opens the door, I will come in and eat with him, and he with me" (Revelation 3:20).

The exquisite coloring, blending of light, and detail give eloquent exposition to the text. The painting portrays the moment when a soul's destiny hangs in the balance as divine love waits upon human reluctance. Oil and color become an evangelistic call to decision. On the canvas the artist has portrayed the door of the human heart, barred with nails and rusty hinges, knotted with creeping ivy, the threshold overgrown with weeds. Jesus is garbed as prophet, priest, and king. He bears the light that penetrates the darkness. His face radiates hope. His expression reveals tenderness and love.

Christ stands at the door of each person's heart, seeking admission. Let us welcome this triumphant Warrior, the King of glory, to our hearts and lives. May we with the psalmist of old know him as our Sovereign and enthrone him without a rival.

Lord Jesus, I open wide the door of my heart for you to live and reign within my life.

CHAPTER 31

Our Light and Salvation

PSALM 27

> *The LORD is my light and my salvation.*
> (27:1a)

THIS FIRST VERSE OF Psalm 27 has long been a favorite quotation for Christian witness. The psalmist does not say that the Lord gives light, but that he *is* our light; not that he gives salvation, but that he *is* our salvation.

The world without Christ is one of darkness, groping and lost. Jesus is the Light that dispels the world's spiritual darkness. Before the miracle at Bethlehem, the world was without light and hope. But Jesus came from heaven to be our Light and hope. He is the Light of the world, who came to be the Light of every life. As our Light, he illumines the soul with an intensity even greater than the sun's. He casts no shadows, no clouds can obscure him, and no night can eclipse him from shining upon and within us.

"The Lord is my Light" is the motto of Oxford University, inscribed in Latin at that great seat of learning: *Dominus illuminatio mea.* May it also be the theme of our lives, inscribed upon our hearts. As our Light, the Lord takes us from the shady to the sunny side of life; he guides so that we may follow in his path. Let our prayer ever be that of John Newman:

> *Lead, kindly Light, amid the encircling gloom.*
> *Lead thou me on!*
> *The night is dark, and I am far from home;*
> *Lead thou me on!*
> *Keep thou my feet; I do not ask to see*
> *The distant scene: one step enough for me.*

"The LORD is my salvation" is the joyful witness of the psalmist. "Salvation" is one of the most sacred terms in Scripture. It concerns everyone, for we have all sinned and will perish unless we receive God's loving offer of salvation. What a comprehensive blessing salvation bestows. It brings deliverance from the guilt of sin, from its dominion, from its curse, from its punishment, and ultimately from its very existence.

For those of us on the other side of Calvary from the psalmist there is even greater meaning in his reference to "the Lord" as the source of our salvation. We know something of the costliness and the infinite love that provided for our salvation. We are heirs of John 3:16: "For God so loved the world that he gave his one and only Son, that whoever believes in him shall not perish but have eternal life."

Imagine knowing of Milton, but not as a poet; or Michelangelo, but not as a sculptor; or Beethoven, but not as a composer. Just as it is possible to know of these great people of history without knowing their real genius that has so immeasurably enriched our cultures, so it is possible to know about Christ but miss knowing him as Savior.

The discovery of the use of chloroform saved the world from more pain than any other single medical breakthrough at that time. Someone asked Sir James Simpson, its discoverer, "What do you regard as your greatest discovery?" Instead of the expected answer, Simpson replied, "My greatest discovery was Jesus Christ as my Savior."

In our preceding chapter we referred to the painting by Holman Hunt, *The Light of the World,* that portrays Christ knocking at the door and awaiting an answer from within. A critic, viewing the painting, said to the artist: "Lovely painting, Mr. Hunt, but you've forgotten something. That door upon which the Master is knocking – is it ever to be opened? You've forgotten to put a knob on the door." Hunt smiled and said, "My friend, that door on which the Master is knocking is not just an ordinary door. It is the door to the human heart. It needs no knob, for it can only be opened from within."

When we have opened the doors of our hearts to Christ, he becomes our Light and salvation, flooding our lives with his radiance and transforming power.

Lord Jesus, thank you for being my Light and salvation.

CHAPTER 32

Our Strength

PSALM 27, CONTINUED

> *The LORD is the strength of my life.*
> (27:1b, KJV)

HE WHO IS OUR Light and who saves us also keeps us. He is our strength, making us adequate for the testings, temptations, and tasks of life.

The psalmist refers to enemies who seek to destroy him. He is beset by those who "advance against me to devour my flesh" (v. 2). He describes himself as being in grave danger from his foes, who besiege him and war against him (vv. 2-3). But with the Lord as his strength, he confidently declares, "Of whom shall I be afraid?" (v. 1).

The Bible is a book of battles, as mirrored in the psalms. Plato reminds us that "Only the dead have seen the end of war." The Christian is called into spiritual battle. We, like David, face a deadly foe. Satan seeks to destroy our souls. Our hearts and minds and flesh are battlefields of spiritual forces. Our own strength will not suffice. But we will be victorious when we can say with the psalmist, "The LORD is the strength of my life" (KJV).

Our own weakness is implied in the affirmation of the psalmist. Self-sufficient people cannot understand or experience the sustaining grace of this promise; they have never learned their own need of the Lord's strength. We learn our weakness as we seek to do God's work, compelled to acknowledge the Lord's own edict: "Without me you can do nothing." We find our weakness when we come to the time of suffering, needing the comfort and sustaining presence of our Lord. Our weakness impinges upon us again as we seek to grow in grace, finding it hard to go a step forward without two steps backward.

We surely find our weakness in the hour of temptation. We all have our tender points of vulnerability. When Thetis dipped Achilles in the River Styx, she held him by the heel. He was made invulnerable wherever the water touched him, but because his heel was not covered with the water it was vulnerable; Paris shot his arrow into Achilles' heel, and he died. It can even be so with us. We may have an Achilles' heel somewhere, a vulnerable place where the arrow of the devil can strike and defeat us. The psalmist witnesses to the secret of victory that can be ours: "The LORD is the strength of my life."

The psalmist is single-minded; he concentrates his energies on the ultimate priority of his life:

> One thing I ask of the LORD,
>   this is what I seek:
> that I may dwell in the house of the LORD
>   all the days of my life,
> to gaze upon the beauty of the LORD
>   and to seek him in his temple.

(v. 4)

May that be the supreme desire and motivation of our life.

Too often our energies are diffused in many directions and lack sufficient focus and force for life's ultimate needs. People today are inclined to say, "These many things I dabble in," unlike the Apostle Paul who affirmed, "This one thing I do."

"This is what I seek," the psalmist says of his desire. Holy aspirations require resolute action. Likewise, we also need to pray, "Teach me your way, O LORD" (v. 11). Amid the chaos and confusion of our world with its tumult of voices, like the psalmist we need to "Wait for the LORD" (v. 14), in whom we will find our courage and strength.

The prayer and aspiration of the psalmist are echoed in the devotional song of Albert Orsborn:

> *In the secret of thy presence,*
>> *Where the pure in heart may dwell,*
> *Are the springs of sacred service*
>> *And a power that none can tell.*
> *There my love must bring its offering,*
>> *There my heart must yield its praise,*
> *And the Lord will come, revealing*
>> *All the secrets of his ways.*
>
> *Blessed Lord, to see thee truly,*
>> *Then to tell as I have seen,*
> *This shall rule my life supremely,*
>> *This shall be the sacred gleam.*
> *Sealed again is all the sealing,*
>> *Pledged again my willing heart,*
> *First to know thee, then to serve thee,*
>> *Then to see thee as thou art.*

Lord Jesus, let me behold your beauty, and then let it be reflected in my life.

CHAPTER 33

"The Splendor of His Holiness"

PSALM 29

> Worship the LORD in the splendor of his holiness.
> (29:2b)

WHEN WE SEEK TO define the attributes of God, they do not fit comfortably into our human analogies and metaphors. God's holiness exceeds the bounds of human vocabulary in our attempts at definition. Holiness has been the topic of innumerable expositions and has often been the source of theological differences of interpretation, leading even to the establishment of splintered denominations. Here the psalmist provides an appropriate matching word when he speaks of the *splendor* of God's holiness. Splendor can be defined as "dazzling brightness, magnificence, grandeur." One of the traditional hymns of the church speaks of God as "pavilioned in splendor." Thus the terms "splendor" and "holiness" are compatibly yoked together in this psalm of David.

"Splendor" is one of the favorite superlatives employed by biblical writers in reference to the ineffable glory of God. No less than four times in Psalms the word is wedded to "majesty" in reference to God (Psalms 45:3; 96:6; 104:1; 145:5). And no less than three times in the Bible the people of God are called to "Worship the LORD in the splendor of his holiness" (1 Chronicles 16:29; Psalms 29:2; 96:9). In his attempt to describe the indescribable event that took place on the Mount of Transfiguration, Luke employs this superlative in reference to Moses and

Elijah, who had come from the courts of heaven, saying that "they appeared in glorious splendor" (Luke 9:30). And we should not be surprised that the Apostle Paul, when writing of the Lord's Second Coming, speaks of "the splendor of his coming" (2 Thessalonians 2:8). Appropriately, in God's Word splendor is wedded with holiness and the majesty and glory of God.

The matter of holiness is highly important to God: the word is found some 650 times in the Bible, not counting words with similar meaning. In the Bible, God's holiness is stressed more than any other attribute. We do not find such frequent reference to God's sovereign name, his loving name, or his powerful name, but again and again God reminds us of his holy name. It is the only attribute thrice repeated: "Holy, holy, holy is the LORD almighty" (Isaiah 6:3; Revelation 4:8).

How marvelous and blessed it is that God, whose great attribute is holiness, deigns to share the splendor of his holiness with us. There are many calls to vocation – some are called to medicine, some to teaching, some to music, some to writing, some to art, some to ministry. God calls men and women to these varied vocations to use the talents with which he endows them. But he calls every believer to the life of holiness: "But just as he who called you is holy, so be holy in all you do; for it is written: 'Be holy, because I am holy'" (1 Peter 1:15-16). The call to be holy is not a call to vocation but a call to character, a call to soul health. It is a call to every child of God, for if we are to dwell in the house of the Lord all the days of our lives, we must be like him in character so as to worship him in the splendor of holiness.

The old Authorized Version of the Bible renders this text, "Worship the LORD in the beauty of holiness." Indeed, what adorns life with beauty more than holiness? Samuel Brengle defined holiness simply and at the same time profoundly: "Holiness is Christlikeness" – being conformed to his love, his purity, his character. When we sing Albert Orsborn's devotional prayer, "Let the beauty of Jesus be seen in me," are we not praying that we will be a holy person? Nothing endows the life more with splendor and beauty than that it should be like Christ. Our petition for this blessing has been expressed for us in the words of Charles Wesley:

> He wills that I should holy be;
>   That holiness I long to feel,
> That full divine conformity
>   To all my Savior's righteous will.
>
> Come, Savior, come and make me whole,
>   Entirely all my sins remove;
> To perfect health restore my soul,
>   To perfect holiness and love.

Holy Spirit, let your full work in me be done, that I may worship the Lord in the splendor of holiness.

CHAPTER 34

It's about Time

PSALM 31

> *My times are in your hands.*
> (31:15a)

THE FOUR SECTIONS OF this psalm may well represent the seasons of the soul as the psalmist struggles through tears to triumph. The reader can see the gathering clouds and yet fruitful faith in verses 1-8, feel the chill of winter in the sighing of verses 9-13, sense the promise of spring in the sunlight of verses 14-18, and bask in the summer warmth of praise and promises as verses 19-24 complete the cycle.

Time is sacred. It is a precious gift from God, very life itself. The wise Benjamin Franklin advised, "Do you love life? Then do not squander time, for it is the stuff of which life is made." It has been observed that the most universal slaughter is the killing of time. Thoreau warned against such waste of time, "As if you could kill time without injuring eternity." There is no present like the time. The Apostle Paul urges us to "Redeem the time" (Ephesians 5:16, KJV). Julia Carney has reminded us:

> Little drops of water, little grains of sand,
> Make the mighty ocean and the present land.
> Thus the little minutes, humble though they be,
> Make the mighty ages of eternity.

For each of us God daily deposits into our account of life 86,400 fleeting seconds, 1,400 precious minutes, and 24 shining hours. No time is carried over from the previous day or put into credit for the next day. It is ours to invest or to waste. It never returns. As Bill and Gloria Gaither have lyricized, "Yesterday's forever gone; tomorrow may never come; but we have this moment, today."

As the psalmist progresses from trouble to trust and triumph, he exclaims: "My times are in your hands." The Hebrew word for "time," *eth,* is variously interpreted as seasons, circumstances, life-stages, or destiny. In other words, our "times" represent all aspects of our life. The outcome of the believer's life is not dictated by chance or circumstance. He lives under the providential guidance of his Lord to whom he has committed his life.

When with the psalmist we affirm, "My times are in your hands," time becomes not a tyrant, but a friend. Professor Time, a most venerable pedagogue, teaches his lessons well. With the Lord's guidance, time can be for us a corrector of errors, a tester of truth, a healer of sorrow, and the one preacher to whom all must listen.

All the seasons of life are in the hands of the One who controls –

- the precise timing of the tides,
- the phases of the moon,
- the migratory flight of birds,
- the cycle of the seasons,
- the course of the stars.

Surely the Governor of the universe, who has set the clock of creation on its cosmic courses, is able to guide our frail and finite lives on their courses so that we will not be erring or erratic, lone or lost.

Robert Browning alludes to verse 15 in his familiar lines:

Grow old along with me!
The best is yet to be,
The last of life for which the first was made.
Our times are in his hand
Who saith, "A whole I planned,
Youth shows but half;
Trust God: see all, nor be afraid!"

Indeed, the best is always "yet to be" when our times are in God's care and keeping.

Eternal God, I place the short earthly seasons of my life in your mighty and loving hands.

CHAPTER 35

The Joyful Heart

PSALM 32

> *Blessed is he*
> *whose transgressions are forgiven,*
> *whose sins are covered.*
> (32:1)

PSALM 32 IS A joyful beatitude sung by the pardoned sinner. It is one of the seven penitential psalms, believed to have been written just after Psalm 51, following David's sin of adultery and murder, and his confession and restoration.

Augustine had this psalm written on the wall opposite his bed during his last sickness. He had experienced sin's disgust and disillusionment. His early life of wanton indulgence and licentious living had been forgiven. The joy of liberation from sin and the reality of forgiveness was his comfort as he was about to depart this life.

In his opening words the psalmist reminds us who is really blessed and truly happy in life. Most people judge by outward appearances. Many in the world measure a person's "blessings" by their portfolio of assets, or by their success in their profession, or by the education and learning they have acquired, or by uninterrupted good health. But one may possess all these and still have an emptiness within one's life. The psalmist sees through the masquerade of outward appearance and pronounces that person blessed who has received God's forgiveness.

The psalmist uses four words for the evils God forgives in life. The first is "transgression," which means passing over a boundary, doing what is prohibited. It is disregarding God's moral "no trespassing" signs. It is stepping across the line drawn between right and wrong.

The second word, "sin," means missing the mark in life, failing to do what God requires. It was said that there were three stages in the career of a brilliant youth who never fulfilled his promise. First it was said of him, "He will do something." Then people said, "He could do something if he would." Finally, it was said of him, "He could have done something." John Greenleaf Whittier expressed it poignantly:

> For of all sad words of tongue or pen,
> The saddest are these: "It might have been!"

The psalmist's third word, "iniquity," refers to moral distortion and perversion. It is the life turned away from its proper course.

"Guile," the fourth word, refers to fraud, deceit, and untruthfulness. When God forgives, he cleanses the life from falsehood and deception.

For each of these evils or types of sin, God has a cure. Transgression is forgiven, sin is covered, iniquity is not imputed, and guile is taken away.

Only when the psalmist confessed his sin to God did he experience forgiveness and joy. He tells us that when he kept silent, instead of joy he had "groaning" and his "strength was sapped" (vv. 3-4). His gloom turned to joy when he ceased trying to "cover up my iniquity" and said, "I will confess my transgressions to the LORD." The result: the Lord "forgave the guilt of my sin" (v. 5).

In human jurisprudence, the term "double jeopardy" refers to the law that a person cannot be tried twice for the same offense. If he is tried once and acquitted, he cannot be tried again. This same principle is true on a much higher scale in divine jurisprudence. Christ paid the penalty for our sins. When we accept his forgiveness, there can be no further penalty for that which he has forgiven. Our sin is "covered," never again to be brought up against us.

The psalmist speaks of the care of God for us: "I will instruct you and teach you in the way you should go; I will counsel you and watch over you" (v. 8). God is not only the One who forgives us; he is also our teacher and guide. Nathaniel Niles was inspired by the Authorized Version's rendering of this verse, "I will guide thee with mine eye," to compose this hymn of trust:

> *Precious promise God hath given*
> *To the weary passerby,*
> *All the way from earth to Heaven:*
> *I will guide thee with mine eye.*
> *When temptations almost win thee,*
> *And thy trusted watchers fly,*
> *Let this promise ring within thee:*
> *I will guide thee with mine eye.*

As with the psalmist, let the joy of your forgiveness overflow my heart in praise.

CHAPTER 36

"Rejoice in the Lord"

PSALM 32, CONTINUED

> Rejoice in the LORD and be glad.
>
> (32:11a)

THE FINAL VERSE OF Psalm 32 is a call to jubilation. Christians are to exude a holy hilarity – to "Rejoice in the LORD and be glad!" We follow the One who said he came that his joy might be in us and that we might have abundant life.

Such joy belongs to those who "are upright in heart" (v. 11b). They are called upon to sing in their rejoicing. Songwriter Mary Servoss was inspired by this verse to write her lines:

> Be glad in the Lord and rejoice,
>   All ye that are upright in heart;
> And ye that have made him your choice,
>   Bid sadness and sorrow depart.

> Though darkness surround you by day,
>   Your sky by the night be o'ercast,
> Let nothing your spirit dismay,
>   But trust till the danger is past.

> Rejoice, rejoice!
> Be glad in the Lord and rejoice!

We may become ecstatic during a sports event, but we often refrain from expressing our joy in the Lord. The psalmist calls us to give voice to our felicity in Christ – rejoice, be glad, sing! Someone once pointed to a man as a Christian whose face was always a picture of gloominess. Another responded, "No; God does not write with such an illegible hand." Ours should be an unbounded, infectious joy in the Lord.

The "upright in heart" possess the joy of the Lord. Sin and moral failure rob us of joy by coming between us and the Lord who is our source of joy. In Paul's list of the fruit of the Spirit (Galatians 5:22-23), joy is the runner-up virtue to love. In fact, we can't have one without the other. The love of God causes joy to overflow in our life.

François Fenelon (1651-1715) in his classic writing, *Christian Perfection,* speaks of the hundredfold happiness of the person fully given over to God. He relates that those on the outside miss the great freedoms of the faith – freedom from stifling self-absorption, from the one-upmanship scheming and insecure systems of the world. He parses the joys of Christian living as the joy of a growing power to do the right, the joy of a peaceful conscience, and the joy of "seeing the light grow in our hearts."

A fable is told of a big dog who saw a little dog chasing his tail and asked, "Why are you chasing your tail?" Said the puppy, "I have learned that the best thing for a dog is happiness and that happiness is in my tail. Therefore, I am chasing my tail, and when I catch it I will have happiness." Said the old dog, "My son, I too have paid attention to our world and have formed some opinions. I too have judged that happiness is a fine thing for a dog, and that happiness is in my tail. I have noticed, however, that when I chase it, it keeps running away from me. But when I go about my business, it comes after me."

Many relentlessly pursue happiness or joy as an end in it-self. They find it to be elusive, always just beyond them. But Christians who "go about their business" doing God's will and work have the joy of the Lord following them wherever they go.

Lord, our source of joy, help me so to live that your joy will radiate from my life.

CHAPTER 37

"Taste and See"

PSALM 34

> *Taste and see that the* LORD *is good.*
> (34:8)

THE JOY OF THE Lord overflows in the life of the psalmist in this psalm. David extols the Lord for his deliverance and an-swer to prayer (vv. 1-7). He exclaims, "His praise will always be on my lips" (v. 1). His exuberance in the Lord makes him want to share with others the joy he has found. His words of invita-tion echo through the centuries: "Taste and see that the LORD is good."

David was one of the most talented persons in the Bible. He was a musician, composer, writer, warrior, statesman. But we do not find him saying to his children, Come and I will teach you how to play the harp, how to compose music, how to write a poem, how to handle the sword or the bow, or how to administer the policy of the state. Rather, in this psalm, we hear him say, "Come, my children, listen to me; I will teach you the fear of the Lord" (v. 11).

Knowledge of God transcends all other learning. A relationship with God surpasses all other joys of life. Such a treasure cannot be kept to ourselves. David knows that any who call upon the Lord will also discover his goodness. The invitation "Taste and see that the Lord is good" has been going forth throughout the whole Christian era. It has been the theme of the evangelist, the burden of the missionary, the joyous witness of every child of God. Charles Wesley adapted this text to a hymn verse:

> O that the world would taste and see
>   The riches of his grace;
> The arms of love that compass me
>   Would all mankind embrace.
> His glorious righteousness I show,
>   His saving truth proclaim;
> 'Tis all my business here below
>   To cry: Behold the Lamb!

William Gladstone, the renowned Prime Minister of Great Britain, was preparing an important speech one morning that was to be delivered that day to Parliament. Early that morning, he heard a timid knock on his door at No. 10 Downing Street in London. He opened the door to a boy whose confidence and friendship he had earlier won. The boy said, "Mr. Gladstone, my brother is dying. Will you please come and show him the way to heaven?" Leaving his important political work for the most important work any Christian can do, Gladstone soon arrived at the bedside of the dying boy and led him to the Savior. Returning to his office, Gladstone wrote at the bottom of the speech he was preparing, "I am today the happiest man in England!"

For every Christian, there is no more important work in all the world than sharing our faith. And there is no greater joy than that of seeing another finding the grace and goodness of Jesus Christ. Let us, by our faithful lives and witness, invite others to "Taste and see that the LORD is good."

Dear Lord, help me to be a faithful daily witness for you.

CHAPTER 38

"Do Not Fret"

PSALM 37

> *Do not fret because of evil men.*
> (37:1)

LUTHER SAID OF PSALM 37, "The sum of this psalm is to learn patience." Its counsel comes to us from the latter years of David, who acknowledges, "Now I am old" (v. 25), so that its insights come from his long and varied experience as well as his trust in God.

"Do not fret because of evil men" (v. 1a). Can any of us claim exemption from this problem? Have we not all gone through times of fuming, fretting, fulminating, and frustration because of people's wrongdoing, their harmful attitudes and actions? Three times the psalmist repeats: "Do not fret" (vv. 1, 7, 8), underscoring the importance of these words. Although circumstances are quite different today, the basic problem of fretting because of wrong done by others is still prevalent today.

We tend to fret when we encounter people who abuse their power or authority, who are insensitive, inconsistent, hypocritical, careless, irresponsible, exploitative, selfish, or lacking integrity. The temptation in our fretting is to become critical or cynical, with the result that we may become resentful and vindictive, compromising our own spiritual lives and influence. The psalmist intimates this in his admonishment, "Refrain from anger . . . do not fret – it leads only to evil" (v. 8). Fretting over the evil of others can lead to evil on the fretter's part.

The psalm also counsels us not to fret over the prosperity of the wicked (v. 7). The prosperity and good fortune of the wicked is one of life's great riddles. Sometimes we may feel like Pompey, who said when defeated by Caesar, "There is a mist over the eye of Providence." Life around us is full of seeming inequalities, inequities, injustices. It is enough to make the ordinary person fret! But, of course, the person of God is not an ordinary person. He or she is possessed of an extraordinary faith and stabilizing power.

Christians do not fret because we see earthly comparisons in the light of eternity. Our earthly life is only a preface to the ending pages of the exciting chapters of eternity God has for us. We are destined to reign with Christ forever.

The psalmist presents a threefold prescription for the cure

of fretting. The first is faith: "Trust in the LORD" (v. 3). We must keep our eyes upon Jesus and less upon others. Then the things and problems of this world, in the words of the chorus by Helen Lemmel, "will grow strangely dim in the light of his glory and grace." The second prescribed cure is this: "Delight yourself in the LORD" (v. 4). Our delight, our pleasure, our satisfaction, our fulfillment are in the Lord. The words of a song express it well: "All my lasting joys are found in Thee,/Jesus, thou art everything to me."

The final prescription that we take to build up our resistance against fretting is commitment: "Commit your way to the LORD" (v. 5). Commitment to the Lord frees us from commitment to our comfort zones, self-gratification, and self-centered expectations of life. When we are truly committed to the Lord, he becomes the priority and motivation of our life, and the external things will be seen in the perspective of his grace and goodness.

Lord, who stilled the sea's raging storm, give me your calm and peace.

CHAPTER 39

Song of Deliverance

PSALM 40

> *He lifted me out of the slimy pit,*
> *out of the mud and mire;*
> *he set my feet on a rock*
> *and gave me a firm place to stand.*
>
> (40:2)

PSALM 40 IS A BALLAD, a song of human experience that speaks to every person who has shared its desperation and deliverance. It was composed to be sung, as the title indicates: "for the director of music." Its theme has inspired the composing of songs through the years. Black slaves in America paraphrased its words as they identified with its expression of hope for spiritual and social salvation:

> *He took my feet from the miry clay.*
> *Yes, He did.*
> *And placed them on the rock to stay.*
> *Yes, He did.*

"He lifted me out of the slimy pit" is an apt description of the situation of someone in the grip of sin. The familiar "miry clay" of the Authorized Version conveys the suggestion of the clinging quality of clay. As we ponder this psalm we should underline in our thinking its metaphors of "slimy pit," "mud and mire," which speak of our condition before "He set my feet on a rock, and gave me a firm place to stand" (v. 2). There could not be a greater contrast between mud and rock, or between a "slimy pit" and "a firm place to stand," just as there cannot be a greater contrast between our condition of sin and of salvation.

When we consider what Christ has done for us, what he has saved us from, we are impelled to sing our songs of deliverance and praise. Christian folk are a singing folk, and the world has resounded with the music that has poured forth from hearts redeemed from the pit of destruction. Church hymnals are replete with the joyful songs the Lord has put in the hearts of the redeemed. Music is the language of the emotions and soul, a vehicle of our praise. Indeed, the Lord puts "a new song in our mouth" (v. 3) – a song of joy, of deliverance, of praise, of worship.

"He inclined unto me, and heard my cry" (v. 1, KJV) extols the psalmist. "Inclined" suggests a bending down, a condescension, a stooping. That is what God did for us in Jesus Christ. In his book *Miracles,* C. S. Lewis writes graphically of this divine condescension, of God coming down "from the heights of absolute being into time and space, down into humanity . . . down to the very roots and sea-bed of the Nature He has created":

> He goes down to come up again and bring the whole ruined world up with Him. One has the picture of a strong man stooping lower and lower to get himself underneath some great complicated burden. He must stoop in order to lift, he must almost disappear under the load before he incredibly straightens his back and marches off with the whole mass swaying on his shoulders.

It was none other than God himself, the Creator and Sovereign of the universe, who "inclined unto me and heard my cry." He stooped down, he condescended to become my Savior, my Helper, my Friend.

"He brought me up also out of an horrible pit, out of the miry clay" (KJV), testifies the psalmist. These graphic terms indicate how utterly desperate and helpless was our condition and how great is the salvation God has given us. Sin was a horrible pit and miry clay for each of us. We were trapped, held in its power, helpless and unable to escape. But God delivered us. He brought us up and out of sin's entrapment. Indeed, he has given to us a jubilant song of deliverance.

Dear Redeemer, thank you for lifting me out of the pit of sin, setting my feet on the rock of salvation, and putting a new song in my heart.

CHAPTER 40

Numberless Blessings

PSALM 40, CONTINUED

> *Many, O LORD my God,*
> *are your wonderful works which you have done . . .*
> *they are more than can be numbered.*
> (40:5, NKJV)

WITH THE PSALMIST, WE exultantly witness to having been rescued from a pit and lifted out of miry clay to a rock. Not only has the Lord rescued us from the clutches of sin, but he has put a new song in our heart. No wonder the psalmist sang of the many wonderful works and thoughts of God toward us, which are "more than can be numbered."

It would be a salutary exercise for our souls to list the works and thoughts of God toward us that come to mind. Indeed, when we start to count our blessings, with the psalmist we find that they are numberless in their grace and goodness to us. Fanny Crosby's song has led many Christians to do just that, to praise the Lord for his numberless blessings:

> *A wonderful Savior is Jesus, my Lord,*
> *A wonderful Savior to me;*
> *He hideth my soul in the cleft of the rock*
> *Where rivers of pleasure I see.*
>
> *A wonderful Savior is Jesus, my Lord,*
> *He taketh my burden away;*

He holdeth me up and I shall not be moved,
  He giveth me strength as my day.

With numberless blessings each moment he crowns,
  And, filled with his goodness divine,
I sing in my rapture: O glory to God
  For such a redeemer as mine!

(1890)

It should excite our minds to recall the wondrous things God has done for us. There is the wonder of his creation and all the bounty and beauty of planet earth so extravagantly bestowed upon us. There is the blessing of the inexhaustible riches of his Word to us. And there is the matchless blessing of Christ himself and his salvation. There is the precious presence of the Holy Spirit within and among us. There is the blessing of family, friends, models, and mentors in our Christian pilgrimage. Indeed, we are spiritually wealthy beyond reckoning. These and other innumerable blessings received from the heart and hand of God give us cause to look forward with eager expectation to the unimaginable blessings yet to come. The Apostle Paul, in such a mood, was led to exclaim: "No eye has seen, no ear has heard, no mind has conceived what God has prepared for those who love him" (1 Corinthians 2:9).

When we ponder and then praise God for what he has done, we soon realize that we can never repay the immeasurable debt of love we owe. In loving gratitude we give our life and our all in return, which then, according to God's grace, becomes the means for even further numberless blessings. We can never out-give God!

Verses 6-7 of this psalm are quoted in Hebrews 10:7 as a prophecy of the Messiah. It is Christ who speaks to us from this psalm, prophetically declaring: "Here I am, I have come." He was not "sent" but came voluntarily to be our Savior. It is he who testifies of his divine purpose in the plan of God: "I desire to do your will" (v. 8), and he gives witness to his servanthood in verses 6-10.

This great psalm closes with a prayer with which we identify. We too confess: "Yet I am poor and needy; may the LORD think of me." The sea of life is great and often turbulent, and our lifeboat is so small. But we too with the psalmist can acknowledge: "You are my help and my deliverer" (v. 17).

Thank you, God, for blessings beyond my ability to count, and for untold blessings yet to come.

CHAPTER 41

Thirsting for God

PSALM 42

> *As the deer pants for streams of water,*
> *so my soul pants for you, O God.*
> *My soul thirsts for God, for the living God.*
> (42:1-2)

THE PSALMIST, WHO LIVED close to the outdoors and its wild creatures, would have seen deer bounding over the mountains and panting for the clear water of the mountain brooks. The animal's compelling thirst, convulsive breath, palpitating heart, and anguished eye for him form a picture that symbolized his intense longing and desperate need for God.

Many today pant after success, position, possessions, wealth, fame, sex, drugs – the things of the world. The psalmist thirsted for the living God. This is the elemental need of the soul. Jesus promises: "Blessed are those who hunger and thirst for righteousness, for they will be filled" (Matthew 5:6). Can we say in the unforgettable language of the psalmist: "As the deer pants for streams of water, so my soul thirsts for you, O God"?

Augustine gave this longing memorable expression in his prayer: "O God, our hearts are restless until they find their rest in thee." There is a deep thirst of the soul that no earthly spring can slake. There are hungers that no earthly bread can satisfy. God alone can fulfill the deepest longings and needs of the spirit. He alone can still the restlessness of the soul. Without him we are like fish out of water, birds without air.

Christ is to our souls what water is to our bodies – an absolute necessity for life and sustenance, and the satisfaction of our most intense longings. God gives this invitation to humanity: "Come, all you who are thirsty, come to the waters" (Isaiah 55:1).

The final invitation in the Word of God is the same: "Whoever is thirsty, let him come; and whoever wishes, let him take the free gift of the water of life" (Revelation 22:17). Jesus declared that he is the Living Water: "Whoever drinks the water I give him will never thirst. Indeed, the water I give him will become in him a spring of water welling up to eternal life" (John 4:14). He has promised there will come a time in his kingdom when his people will be with him, and "never again will they thirst" (Revelation 7:16).

May we, like the psalmist, have a deep craving for fellowship with God, an intense eagerness to know him, a soul longing for God himself. May the living God be our most passionate quest, our heart's most fervent yearning. With the seventeenth-century song writers Nahum Tate and Nicholas Brady, in their paraphrase of this psalm, we would pray:

As pants the hart for cooling streams
    When heated in the chase,
So longs my soul, O God, for Thee,
    And Thy refreshing grace.

For Thee, my God, the living God,
    My thirsty soul doth pine;
Oh, when shall I behold Thy face,
    Thou Majesty Divine?

Why restless, why cast down, my soul?
    Hope still, and thou shalt sing
The praise of Him who is thy God,
    Thy health's eternal Spring.

(1696)

Living God, quench the deep thirstings of my soul.

CHAPTER 42

Intimations of Immortality

PSALM 42, CONTINUED

> *Deep calls to deep.*
> (42:7)

THE AUTHOR OF THIS psalm is in deep distress. Tears are his portion day and night (v. 3). In his loneliness he searches the archives of his soul and remembers a former uninhibited time "with shouts of joy" (v. 4). Although in this moment of depression the voice of God is muted, he cannot forget the God of his past experience. It can often be a therapy of the soul to remember our experiences with God in the past.

He addresses his soul: "Why are you downcast, O my soul? Why so disturbed within me?" (v. 5). Why do we experience such inner distress at times? There are no easy answers. Some experiences remain inscrutable to human understanding. But the end of human distress comes not from understanding, but from God himself – "Put your hope in God" (v. 5).

Somewhere in the subterranean chambers of his soul the psalmist hears a call to a deeper, fuller life. He reaches out to depths beyond his finiteness and frailty and finds those depths reaching out to him in his time of need: "Deep calls to deep" (v. 7). There are times when we may be called upon to pass through the wilderness of the soul and will need to echo the prayer of Bernard of Clairvaux: "O my God, the deep of my profound misery calls to the deep of your infinite mercy." The deep of God's love and revelations calls to the depths of human need.

Surely, the amazing phenomena of our world speak to us of the Creator behind them. The profuse and profound thoroughfares of intergalactic space, the swirling worlds and infinite cosmos, speak of the hidden Creator behind it all. The love and goodness of God are mediated through words and the Word, through sunsets and seasons, through the simple trust of a child and the helping hand of a friend. Above all, the fathomless deep of Calvary calls to the deep of our spiritual need.

All around us God has put intimations of immortality. Within us resides an unrelenting intuition to see beyond temporal horizons, to press beyond the limits of the finite. A sense of destiny haunts us. Eternal forces ripple in our blood. Immortal calls echo in our ears. Sublime visions flash upon the screens of our imagination. Eternity beckons us as its deep calls to the depths God has put in our souls. Wordsworth clothed this truth in elegant language:

> *But trailing clouds of glory do we come*
> *From God, who is our home;*
> *Heaven lies about us in our infancy!*

Like Francis Thompson, we too are haunted by the distant sound of "a trumpet from the hid battlements of eternity." Where deep calls to deep in our communion with God, we find there the balance, the rhythm of the spiritual life between contemplation and our daily living. Contemplation on the deep things of God is the spring, and action is the stream. In contemplation we learn to fine-tune our awareness of God's presence and his will for us. Thomas Merton summarizes this truth in his statement: "The only thing that really matters is for love to spring inexhaustibly from the infinite abyss of Christ and of God."

In prayer, we have the nearest approach to God, the noblest exercise of the soul, and the most exalted use of our faculties. The culmination of our being is that of union with God through Christ, when the deep of our soul has linked with the deep of the reality of God.

Eternal God, help me to tune in to the deep of your presence and revelations of grace.

CHAPTER 43

Songs in the Night

PSALM 42, CONTINUED

> *By day the LORD directs his love,*
> *at night his song is with me.*
> (42:8)

THOSE WHO HAVE SEEN the classic musical, *Phantom of the Opera*, will recall the hauntingly beautiful melody and the words:

> *I compose the music of the night. . . .*
> *Close your eyes and let music set you free.*
> *Only then can you belong to me.*

Let your darker side give in to the power of the music that I write,
the power of the music of the night.

In a deeper and spiritual sense this is the experience of God's people. God is the Composer of the music of the night, music that affirms we belong to him and that sets us free from the darkness.

The psalmist witnessed to such a providence in his life: "By day the LORD directs his love, at night his song is with me." This golden promise is repeated again in Psalm 77:6: "I remembered my songs in the night," and by Isaiah in a time of crisis: "You shall have a song as in the night" (Isaiah 30:29, NRSV).

Everyone knows well the story of Job in the Bible. He experienced the saddest woes of any of its characters – the loss of his health, his beloved children, and all that was dear to him. Job's whole world came tumbling down upon him. In that experience, his friend Elihu came to him and reminded him of the radiant truth that God "gives songs in the night" (Job 35:10).

And what was the song in the night that God gave to Job? When the black curtain of catastrophe fell over his soul, in his darkest hour a shaft of brilliant sunlight broke through his midnight sky, and he gave to the centuries the sublime song, as incorporated by Handel in his immortal *Messiah*: "I know my Redeemer lives!" (Job 19:25). Job was but the forerunner of a great company to whom God gave songs in the night, hymns born in the crucible of adversity.

Many know the story of Joni Eareckson Tada and the marvelous world ministry the Lord has given her. But her faith and that ministry were forged out of a dark night of her soul. Joni, a quadriplegic at age 17 from a diving accident, found her condition impossible to reconcile with faith in a loving God. She shares: "In one of those mad, midnight moments during my long convalescence, I came up with a song. Since I couldn't jump out of bed and get a pad of paper and pen, I carefully pondered and memorized each phrase as it came. When the whole poem was complete in my head, I didn't feel so depressed about the will of God." This is the song that God gave to her in that midnight hour, one that has since been recorded and has blessed many lives.

> *I have a piece of china,*
> *A pretty porcelain vase.*
> *It holds such lovely flowers,*
> *Captures everybody's gaze.*
> *But fragile things do slip and fall*
> *As everybody knows,*
> *And when my vase came crashing down,*
> *Those tears began to flow.*
>
> *My life was just like china,*
> *A lovely thing to me,*
> *Full of porcelain promises*
> *Of all that I might be.*
> *But fragile things do slip and fall*
> *As everybody knows,*
> *And when my life came crashing down,*
> *Those tears began to flow.*
>
> *Now Jesus is no porcelain prince,*
> *His promises won't break.*
> *His holy Word holds fast and sure,*
> *His love no one can shake.*

So if your life is shattered
    By sorrow, pain, or sin,
His healing love will reach right down
    And make you whole again.

                                                    (1981)

When we go through our night season of the soul, let us listen, for surely we with the psalmist of old will find, "At night his song is with me."

Divine Composer of the songs of the night, teach me to listen so as to know "the power of the music of the night."

CHAPTER 44

Sorrows into Symphonies

PSALM 42, CONTINUED

> *By day the* LORD *directs his love,*
>   *at night his song is with me.*
>   (42:8)

THE LATIN PROVERB, *ad astra per aspera* (to the stars through hardship), becomes the living experience of God's people. The psalmist was going through the turbulence of deep waters as storms swept over him, threatening to engulf him (v. 7). Many of God's children identify with the psalmist in being over-whelmed in a sea of affliction. But we follow One whose power stilled the tempest of the churning Sea of Galilee and who spoke his word of peace to turn the storm into a calm.

Once again we remind ourselves that in this dark season of his soul, the psalmist heard the strains of God's assuring love and care: "at night his song is with me." A Hasidic saying states that there are three ways in which a man expresses his deep sorrow: the man on the lowest level cries; the man on the second level is silent; the man on the highest level turns his sorrow into song. The psalmist, and succeeding generations of God's people, have found that God turns our sorrows into symphonies.

Fanny Crosby's hymns have inspired millions. She was incredibly prolific, composing over 9,000 hymns. She has enriched our singing with such favorites as "Blessed Assurance," "Jesus Keep Me Near the Cross," and "To God Be the Glory." Fanny Crosby did her composing in a perpetual dark night – she was blind. But God lit a light in her mind and soul that enabled her to see and share "rivers of pleasure" and "visions of rapture" that found their way into her songs. God gave her songs in the night that will resonate throughout time.

Soon or late, each of us will come to our night seasons of life. The Bible and the history of God's people remind us that trouble is the common lot of humanity. Pain and suffering wear a thousand guises. Lives may be shattered by accident or disaster. An illness or death may rob us of a beloved, or its dread shadow may be hovering over a loved one. We may be compelled to watch a loved one suffer, to witness mental deterioration of a friend or family member, or to see a promising young life wither and die.

To borrow from Job's story, such a time as these is when the

Sabeans attack, when the lightning strikes, when the Chaldeans raid, when the wind blows with fury against our house. That's when the unforeseen is no longer a theoretical chapter in a book but becomes our personal nightmare. Of such dark and tragic fabric, the tapestry of human life is made. So if the sun shines brightly today, then beware, be prepared, never trust the cease-fires of Satan.

When the road we walk becomes steeper, when the night we endure grows darker, when the load we carry becomes heavier, and when the pain we feel reaches deeper, God has a song in the night just for us. It may not be a traditional lyric set to music. It may come as a precious promise from his Word, as with Job. It may come as a comforting friend, or a mentor. It may come on the wings of an insight that will help us to get through. But in a thousand ways, God comes to his children in their night seasons, with his presence and promise, as a song in the night. This truth has been beautifully woven into a hymn by Anna Russell:

> *There is never a day so dreary,*
> *There is never a night so long,*
> *But the soul that is trusting Jesus*
> *Will somewhere find a song.*

> *Wonderful, wonderful Jesus,*
> *In the heart He implanteth a song:*
> *A song of deliverance, of courage, of strength;*
> *In the heart He implanteth a song.*

Thank you, Lord, for setting our pain to music, for your songs that come to us in the night seasons of our soul.

CHAPTER 45

Our Refuge and Strength

PSALM 46

> God is our refuge and strength.
>
> (46:1)

IN TIMES OF GREAT danger, Martin Luther would say to his friend Melanchthon, "Come, Philip, let us sing the forty-sixth psalm." It is often called "Luther's Psalm," not because he staked any proprietary claims to it, but because he fashioned from the bright gold of its truth his great Reformation hymn, "A Mighty Fortress Is Our God." Psalm 46 inspired the sixteenth-century monk to write a hymn that became the battle song of the Reformation. Succeeding generations of believers would forever after sing:

> A mighty fortress is our God,
>   A bulwark never failing;
> Our helper He, amid the flood
>   Of mortal ills prevailing.

When we come yieldingly into God's presence, we discover his power and peace. We too will find that "God is our refuge and strength, an ever present help in trouble. Therefore we will not fear" (vv. 1-2). There are times and troubles that even our closest loved ones and friends are not able to enter into. But God is "an ever present help in trouble." The word "ever" gives a reassuring emphasis.

When the forecast calls for storms, ships need a sure anchor; buildings, a sure foundation; trees, deep roots. In each case, their survival through the storm depends upon a strong link to that which cannot be moved. The divine Refuge and Strength of Psalm 46 is that anchor and foundation for the Christian.

Faith in God becomes the antidote to fear. With the psalmist, we too can declare amid life's crises, "Therefore we will not fear" (v. 2). Throughout the Bible there are 365 "fear nots" or its equivalent. God has given us one for every day of the year!

An epigram carved over a saloon door on the *Titanic* read: "Not even God can sink this ship." That piece of arrogant blasphemy still rots at the bottom of the Atlantic. Modern people are infected with the myth of self-sufficiency, of autonomy, of being the captain of their own fates. This psalm is an antidote to that fatal illusion. It reminds us that our strength alone is insufficient, that we need God as our refuge and strength for the testings that will surely come our way.

God is all sufficient for the believer, and his power and defense are equal to any emergency. This truth became a reality for Cleveland Indians baseball star Andre Thornton. In 1977, he was driving his wife and two children through the mountain roads of Pennsylvania. They encountered rain that turned to sleet and snow, with high winds. A tragic accident claimed the lives of his wife and daughter.

Andre Thornton recalls: "It was a gut-wrenching time. I felt as though the insides of my body were being torn out. But, even at that moment, the Lord was sufficient. I knew that Christ was there with us in the midst of our most difficult moments. The Lord's strength upheld my son and me and allowed us to go on. The greatest thing I learned in that experience is that God is faithful."

There may well be a storm on the horizon of your life. The promise of this psalm is as faithful today as it was for its author. With Luther, we can confidently sing:

Did we in our own strength confide,
Our striving would be losing.
Were not the right man on our side,
The man of God's own choosing.
Dost ask who that may be?
Christ Jesus, it is he,
Lord Sabaoth his name,
From age to age the same,
And he must win the battle.

(1529)

God, my refuge and my strength, sustain me amid the conflicts and battles of my life.

CHAPTER 46

Re-creating Stillness

PSALM 46, CONTINUED

> *Be still, and know that I am God.*
> (46:10)

DR. THOMAS HOLMES, IN researching the effects of stress, developed a table called "Life Change Units" (LCUs), ascribing numerical values to stressful events. For example, the death of a spouse is assigned 100 points, divorce 73, retirement 45. If a person in a given year scores between 100 and 300, he faces a 50 percent chance of a serious health change. A score of over 300 points foreshadows an 80 percent chance for major health change (disease, surgery, accident, mental illness, etc.) within the next two years.

The psalmist had no such scale of LCUs, but he had an intimate knowledge of shattering experiences. In this psalm he employs dramatic metaphors: "Though the earth give way and the mountains fall into the heart of the sea" (v. 2). He is describing the worst possible devastating events that may befall him, when that which may have seemed most stable and sure crumbles about him.

This psalm became a major source of comfort and courage in the aftermath of the terrorist attacks in America on September 11, 2001, arguably the most tragic day in the history of our country. It was read in televised services, both national and regional, held around the country. As described by the psalmist of his day, those things that had once seemed so secure came tumbling down upon us. In that day of infamy in our nation's history, and since then, we have needed the assuring word of this psalm that God is an ever present help in the time of trouble, and because he is with us we need not fear.

Stressful situations come to each life. Adverse and unsettling circumstances may beset any one of us, or those close to us, at any time – difficult relationships, illness, disease, suffering, death. Some may seem like emotional earthquakes in keeping with the descriptions of the psalmist.

"Therefore we will not fear" is the confident assertion of the psalmist. In contrast to the devastation about him, "There is a river whose streams make glad the city of God" (v. 4). It is the river of God's grace, bringing its fertilizing and sustaining refreshment to the believer. Fanny Crosby in her blindness found such a river and led us to sing with her: "He hideth my soul in the cleft of the rock, where rivers of pleasure I see."

What can we do when potentially shattering experiences come upon us? "Come and see the works of the LORD" (v. 8), counsels the psalmist. When we contemplate the marvelous might and wonderful grace of God, we will take courage and have confidence that he will sustain us amid life's most devastating circumstances.

The psalmist reminds us of the protection of God (vv. 1-3), the presence of God (vv. 4-7), and the power of God (vv. 8-11). We may experience all of these through the re-creating stillness to which he directs us: "Be still, and know that I am God" (v. 10). To "be still" is often the opposite of what we tend to do when hit by stress. We react, become exercised, and get caught up in hurry and worry.

But there is a mighty power in silence. Gravity is a silent

force, yet it holds stars and galaxies in their orbits. Sunbeams make their long journey to earth, unheard by human ear, yet bear an incomputable energy. The dew falls silently, yet brings refreshment and beauty. Nature's mighty miracles are wrought in silence. Noise and confusion come from humankind.

John Oxenham's hymn speaks to us of this silent source of serenity and strength:

Mid all the traffic of the ways,
Turmoils without, within,
Make in my heart a quiet place,
And come and dwell therein.

A little shrine of quietness,
All sacred to thyself,
Where thou shalt all my soul possess,
And I may find myself.

Come occupy my silent place,
And make thy dwelling there!
More grace is wrought in quietness
Than any is aware.

(1917)

Eternal God, lead me beside the still waters where I may find your presence, and myself.

CHAPTER 47

Sin's Tangled Web

PSALM 51

> *Against you, you only, have I sinned*
> *and done what is evil in your sight.*
>
> (51:4)

THIS PSALM FURNISHES OUR souls with the language of devotion in our own seasons of confession and contrition. How many times have we needed to come for cleansing and restoration? How many times have the words of this psalm expressed the need of our own souls?

Thomas à Kempis (1380-1471), in his devotional masterpiece *The Imitation of Christ,* reminds us: "No one is completely free of temptations because the source of temptation is in ourselves. We were born in sinful desire. We will always have temptation because we are sinners who lost our original innocence in the Garden. All of the saints passed through times of temptation and tribulation." This psalm deals with the defeat of David in the subtle and deadly temptation that came to him.

The ascription identifies its occasion and background: "A psalm of David. When the prophet Nathan came to him after David had committed adultery with Bathsheba." To appreciate its powerful message fully, we need to recall the story that gave it birth, as recorded in 2 Samuel, chapters 11 and 12.

At eventide, from his roof, David viewed Bathsheba bathing. The record states, "The woman was very beautiful." Here we see the first step toward his fearful fall. He allowed sin to get his attention, to receive hospitality in his imagination. That led then to the next step – he sought to satisfy the lust he had entertained in his mind: "David sent someone to find out about her. . . . Then David sent messengers to get her. She came to him, and he slept with her."

"The woman conceived and sent word to David, saying, 'I am pregnant.'" The day of reckoning had come. The penalty for adultery in that day was death. Bathsheba's husband, Uriah, was away serving in David's army.

David next attempted to cover up his sin by having his general, Joab, send Uriah to him. Summoned back from the scene of fighting, Uriah was given an audience with David under the pretense of reporting on how the fighting was going. David then told Uriah to go down to his house. The secret design of the king was to get Uriah to spend a night at home so that the child would seem to have been fathered by him. "But Uriah slept at the entrance of the palace." When David was told this, he reproved Uriah, "Why didn't you go home?" The noble character of Uriah was revealed in his answer: while his fellow soldiers were encamped in open fields, he could not go to his house to eat and drink and lie with his wife. David called him to his palace and enticed him to become drunk on the king's wine, but still Uriah did not go home.

We now see to what incredible lengths sin can lead. David next sent a letter to Joab, the commander of the army, by Uriah himself: "Put Uriah in the front line where the fighting is fiercest. Then withdraw from him so he will be struck down and die."

The abominable order was carried out, and David became guilty not only of the sin of adultery but also of the heinous crime of the murder of one of his most noble soldiers. Bath-sheba became David's wife. The record poignantly states: "But the thing that David had done displeased the LORD."

The story behind this psalm of penitence powerfully reminds us, as does the poet Sir Walter Scott: "Oh, what a tangled web we weave,/When first we practice to deceive!" When we give way to sin's enticements, each step leads into greater bondage and nearer to destruction. This account warns us that we dare not flirt with sin. As soon as we take the first step, sin starts to weave its entanglement about us, with each succeeding sin trapping us further in its web of destruction.

Holy God, give me a healthy respect and fear of sin that I may ever cling close to you.

CHAPTER 48

Sin Exposed

PSALM 51, CONTINUED

Surely you desire truth in the inner parts.
(51:6)

IN THE LIGHT OF our unfaithfulness, God's faithfulness shines the brightest. David had forsaken God, but "The LORD sent Nathan the prophet to David" (2 Samuel 12:1). God takes the initiative. It was not David who sent for Nathan the prophet, though he never needed him more. Even when we may try to hide from God, he still seeks us. It was so with Moses as a fugitive in Midian, with Elijah under the juniper tree, with Jonah in the depths of the sea, and with Peter after his denial. The Apostle Paul tells us: "If we are faithless, he will remain faithful" (2 Timothy 2:13).

Nathan relates to David the following story:

> There were two men in a certain town, one rich and the other poor. The rich man had a very large number of sheep and cattle, but the poor man had nothing except one little ewe lamb he had bought. He raised it, and it grew up with him and his children. It shared his food, drank from his cup and even slept in his arms. It was like a daughter to him.
>
> Now a traveler came to the rich man, but the rich man refrained from taking one of his own sheep or cattle to prepare a meal for the traveler who had come to him. Instead, he took the ewe lamb that belonged to the poor man and prepared it for the one who had come to him.
>
> (2 Samuel 12:1-4)

The chronicler records the king's enraged reaction at the fictitious character Nathan had created. "As surely as the LORD lives," he said, "the man who did this deserves to die! He must pay for that lamb four times over, because he did such a thing and had no pity."

Although it is obvious to us that in Nathan's parable, the allusion was to David's sin, the king did not see its application to himself. This illustrates how, when we are out of touch with God, we become blinded to our own sins. We may be filled with righteous indignation at the sins of others, but unable to see our own. In condemning the rich man in the parable, David unwittingly condemned himself.

In one of the most dramatic moments of biblical narrative, Nathan unmasked the true villain. Pointing to the royal sinner, he said, "You are the man!"

The words of the prophet struck David's heart like an arrow. In this moment when God broke through to him, all his palace could not afford relief for his stricken conscience. The king who could command unquestioning allegiance from his subjects was not able to still the voice of God's Spirit or his own outraged conscience. "Then David said to Nathan, 'I have sinned against the LORD.'"

God's Word warns us: "You may be sure that your sin will find you out" (Numbers 32:23). Sin may or may not be exposed, but this verse states a deeper truth – "your sin will find you out." It will register in you; you will get the consequences in yourself. Sin blights the life. It is sand in the machinery of living. The word "evil" is the word "live" spelled backwards. As David found, to pay a lifelong regret for an hour's pleasure is a fool's bargain. For surely sin does find us out, both within ourselves and before others.

The devotional verse of Herbert Booth speaks to the need of our own hearts:

> From thee I would not hide
>   My sin because of fear
> What men may think; I hate my pride,
>   And as I am appear,
> Just as I am, O Lord,
>   Not what I'm thought to be,

Just as I am, a struggling soul
   For life and liberty.

Too often people tend to be most concerned with their image, with how people perceive them. But the story of David's transgression, and its exposure, counsels us to take care of the reality, and the image will take care of itself.

Lord, I come to you as a struggling soul and pray for cleansing from every stain of sin.

CHAPTER 49

Prayer for Pardon

PSALM 51, CONTINUED

> *Wash me, and I will be whiter than snow.*
> (51:7b)

WE LEFT DAVID IN the moment of exposure to his grievous sins of lust, intrigue, adultery, treachery, and murder of his faithful soldier. He had broken five of the ten commandments. Confronted with his heinous sin by Nathan the prophet, he found the hidden scandal now in the open. Struck with the unerring arrow of conviction from God's quiver, he cried out, "I have sinned against the LORD."

The spark of divine grace was rekindled in his heart. God's loving-kindness did not fail, even in David's terrible unfaithfulness. David's conviction then led him to deep contrition, and he prayed for pardon.

"Have mercy on me, O God" was the first plea of David's heart. All he could do was to cast himself upon the mercy of God. We, too, come to God with no merit of our own. We, too, come as guilty sinners with the need to pray for mercy. God seeks us out when we have willfully strayed. He forgives and restores us far beyond our deserving.

David prayed not only for forgiveness, but for a total cleansing. There is an intensity in his words – "have mercy . . . blot out . . . wash away . . . cleanse me" (vv. 1-2). He saw the repugnancy of his sin, not only in society's eyes, but before God. His distress was not only for his sin's terrible consequences, but for its very existence in his inner life, an enemy ever lurking within to destroy him.

We need to see sin for what it is. A commercial advertisement shows us a picture of breathtaking scenery: a velvet hillside of grass, towering palisades, and stately pines along a shimmering sea. The lovely scene makes one desire to be in that place. The commercial subtly suggests that the cigarette in the young man's hand is the key to this magic world of beauty. But, if we look carefully enough, we see the contradiction in the black letters in the white box at the bottom of the page: "Warning: the Surgeon General has determined that cigarette smoking is dangerous to your health."

The truth was not in the scenery, but in the print at the bottom of the page. Truth comes later when doctors treat a poisoned lung. The forbidden fruit may always seem delightful in prospect, for no sin ever presents itself under the guise of evil.

Solicitation to evil always wraps itself in the garment of virtue. But sin is more than a footnote to the rest of life, more than a mere parenthesis in our busy round of everyday activity. When indulged, it takes command, and ultimately it will wreak its havoc and destruction.

The leader with the most monumental influence on Christian theology, from the Apostle Paul until Martin Luther, was Augustine. In early life he was trapped in "the swirling mists of lust and whirlpools of vice." As a wild, wanton, and rebellious youth he deserted God. At first he prayed, "Lord, save me from my sins; but not yet." And back he went to spend his youthful energies in immorality. Again the hollowness of his unholy life convicted him. He prayed again, "Lord, save me from all my sins, except one." And once more he left the place of prayer to indulge in sin. Finally he came back to the God who had created him, and to whom his mother, Monica, had so faithfully prayed for his salvation. Humbly, resolutely, he surrendered his life to the will of God, praying: "Lord, save me from all my sins, and save me now."

That, in essence, was David's penitential cry for pardon and purity. The prayer of Psalm 51 can become our road back to God, as we confess to him our sin and seek his cleansing and restoration.

Holy God, help me to see the enormity of my transgressions, and with the psalmist to pray, "Cleanse me from my sin."

CHAPTER 50

Prayer for Purity

PSALM 51, CONTINUED

> *Create in me a pure heart, O God.*
> (51:10)

SOLZHENITSYN, IN HIS *Gulag Archipelago,* relates an astonishing phenomenon that occurred periodically in the German war
trials. The defendant would clasp his head in his hands, refuse
to make any defense, and from then on ask no concession from
the court. He would say that the presentation of his crimes, re-
vived and once again confronting him, had filled him with
such revulsion that he no longer wanted to live. Solzhenitsyn
writes: "That is the ultimate height a trial can attain: when evil
is so utterly condemned that even the criminal is revolted by
it." Centuries ago Augustine echoed this truth when he wrote,
"The punishment of sin is sin."

David asks God to "Wash away all my iniquity and cleanse
me from my sin" (v. 2). He wants to be rid, once and for all, of
the presence and power of sin within him. Although he has conquered his enemies throughout the land, he himself has been
conquered by sin. Though he wears the crown as Israel's greatest monarch, he has not ruled his own spirit.

In St. Petersburg, Russia, there is a magnificent equestrian
statue of Peter the Great with his hand uplifted, pointing his nation onward toward the sea. Peter was the maker of modern
Russia. In many respects, he well deserved the name "Great."

But he was subject to maniacal outbursts of fury, in one of which he killed his own son. Toward the end of his reign, Peter the Great confessed, "I have conquered an empire, but I was not able to conquer myself."

David prays that God will help him now to conquer the sin, the carnality, the evil that lurks deep in his heart. He acknowledges his problem for what it is – transgressions, iniquity, sin, evil (vv. 1-4). The word "sin" has almost disappeared from serious use in the modern vocabulary. We use such euphemisms as "mistakes," "infractions," "problems," "error," etc. But David prayed, "I know my transgressions, and my sin is always before me."

"Surely I have been a sinner from birth," he says, "sinful from the time my mother conceived me" (v. 5). This psalm addresses our innate depravity. We have all been birthed in iniquity, inheriting our sinful nature from our first parents. From them, the venom of sin entered the bloodstream of humanity. Sin for each of us is archetypal, a constitutional disease, requiring a purging in our heart by the Holy Spirit.

"Create in me a pure heart" is the cry of David as he is confronted with his sin against a holy God. The Hebrew word for create, *bara,* is the same word used in Genesis 1:1 when God created the cosmos. David does not pray to have his nature improved, or amended, but re-created. Eugene Peterson paraphrases this prayer of David: "Give me a clean bill of health. God, make a fresh start in me, shape a Genesis week from the chaos of my life." David prays for a heart inclined toward God instead of sin. God, in his mercy and compassion, granted David's penitential cry for purging and purity.

Purity has been a major concern of our time. We want pure water, free of pollutants. We want pure food, free of poisons.

We want pure air, free of toxicants. We pass legislation and spend great sums to assure purity. We prefer purity to impurity, health to sickness, perfection to imperfection, flawlessness to faultiness, the authentic to the artificial. But when it comes to the spiritual life, many settle for less. God calls us to purity.

Our prayers should lead us to seek not only pardon but also purity. William Law in his classic devotional writing, *A Serious Call to a Devout and Holy Life,* reminds us that "Our lives should be as holy and heavenly as our prayers. It is as great an absurdity to offer up holy prayers without a holy life as it is to live a holy life without prayer." David's prayer of confession revealed his need for purity as well as pardon.

Two centuries ago, Søren Kierkegaard in his classic work on the discipline of self-examination wrote: "Purity of heart is to will one thing." To those who, with all their heart, will pray the prayer of David in this psalm as their one dominant desire, God will give the blessing of a pure heart. It does not come by our effort; rather, it is created by the Holy Spirit.

Alfred Lord Tennyson's Sir Galahad said, "My strength is as the strength of ten/Because my heart is pure." Spiritual power becomes the byproduct of purity of heart.

Create in me a pure heart, O God.

CHAPTER 51

Prayer for the Holy Spirit

PSALM 51, CONTINUED

> *Do not cast me from your presence*
> *or take your Holy Spirit from me.*
> (51:11)

IT IS SAD TO see a house that once hosted the warmth of family life and joys now abandoned. It is sad to come upon a farm that once abounded in fertility now overgrown with weeds. It is sad to see a ship that once proudly plied the oceans now derelict. But the saddest sight of all would be a desolate Christian, no longer rich in divine fellowship, no longer filled with the Spirit and bearing fruit. We need the presence and power of the Holy Spirit to be what God wants us to be, and the greatest loss for a Christian is the loss of the Holy Spirit. David, fearing this more than all else, implores, "Do not cast me from your presence or take your Holy Spirit from me."

David's plea is that of a man suddenly feeling that the foundations of his life are in danger of being swept away. "Take anything else in all my kingdom, but not the one thing that makes life livable! Take not your Holy Spirit from me." To lose the Spirit is to lose the very presence of God in one's life, to lose out in the struggle between good and evil. If the Spirit goes, then gone is the Light to guide us, the Helper to uphold us, the Enabler in our service for God, the source of our peace and joy and the fruit that he creates in our lives. To lose the indwelling presence of the Holy Spirit is of all deprivations the most far-reaching and calamitous.

Spiritual joys had deserted David and left his life empty when he was in sin. The dust had settled upon the strings of his harp because the Spirit within was grieved. But his joy of salvation was restored (v. 12). Then he could pray, "O LORD, open my lips, and my mouth will declare your praise" (v. 15). Nothing so effectively closes the lips of praise as the sense and shame of sin.

Miracle of miracles, we too may experience God's gracious forgiveness and restoration by these same steps back to God. Perhaps we have felt the need for a closer walk with our Lord, a renewing of our commitment and covenant. The prayer song of Will Brant expresses that longing in its spiritual kinship with this great penitential psalm of David:

> When from sin's dark hold thy love had won me,
>   And its wounds thy tender hands had healed,
> As thy blest commands were laid upon me,
>   Growing light my growing need revealed.
> Then I sought the path of consecration
>   When to thee, dear Lord, my vows were given:
> And the joy which came with full salvation
>   Winged my feet and filled my heart with heaven.
>
> But my heart at times with care is crowded,
>   Oft I serve with weak, o'erladen hands,
> And that early joy grows dim and clouded
>   As each day its heavy toll demands.
> Have I ceased from walking close beside thee?
>   Have I grieved thee with an ill-kept vow?

In my heart of hearts have I denied thee?
  Speak, dear Lord, O speak and tell me now.

By the love that never ceased to hold me
  In a bond nor life nor death shall break;
As thy presence and thy power enfold me,
  I would plead fresh covenant to make.
From before thy face, each vow renewing,
  Strong in heart, with purpose pure and deep,
I will go henceforth thy will pursuing,
  With my Lord unbroken faith to keep.

Holy Spirit, come and cleanse and dwell within me, that I may have the joy of salvation and lead others to the Savior.

CHAPTER 52

Steps to Wholeness

PSALM 51, CONTINUED

> *Then I will teach transgressors your ways,*
> *and sinners will turn back to you.*
> (51:13)

DAVID, WHO HAD FOUGHT many enemies in his lifetime, had found in his grievous sin no enemy like an offended conscience, no anguish compared to his self-reproach, no war so fierce as that which rages within the human spirit. It has been said that "nobody buys a little passing pleasure in evil at so dear a rate as a good man."

One of the lessons taught by this psalm is that sin outruns the intention. The celebrated Scarsdale diet doctor murder case supplies a dramatic example. Dr. Herman Tarnover, a man of wealth and celebrity status, could not foresee that what started out as an affair with one of many mistresses would end with his own murder. And for Jean Harris, who enjoyed professional success, an elite social circle, charm, and intelligence, the end would be a protracted and excruciating courtroom ordeal, a shattered career, and a long jail term. Sin has a way of feeding on itself and careening out of control. David experienced this in his sin of adultery with Bathsheba, which ultimately led to his murder of her husband.

We see revealed in this psalm the steps back to God. David's restoration had to begin with acknowledgment of his sin. As long as he sought to cover it up, he would remain unforgiven and outside the will and fellowship of God. "Against you, you only, have I sinned and done what is evil in your sight" (v. 4). To realize that an offense against another human being is a sin against God is one of the profoundest of moral insights.

When we transgress God's moral law, we require the pardon of an almighty and all holy God. With David, we must pray: "Have mercy on me, O God, according to your unfailing love; according to your great compassion . . . blot out my transgressions" (v. 1). When God, in his matchless mercy, forgives, he wipes the slate clean. He "blots out" our sins.

David realized that it was not sufficient to deal with the fruit of his sin; he had to get at the root of it – his sinful nature within. God requires inward purity: "Surely you desire truth in the inner parts" (v. 6). David cried from the depths of his soul: "Cleanse me with hyssop, and I will be clean" (v. 7). The hyssop plant was used in the ritual cleaning of persons healed of leprosy. David likens his sin to a dread leprosy of the soul that needs God's purging.

He prays that no stain of sin will remain in his heart. "Wash me," he pleads, "and I will be whiter than snow" (v. 7). He would not be satisfied to have his heart washed merely as white as snow, because snow can become tainted with earth's impurities. He wants God to wash him "whiter than snow."

In order for God to do his creative work in our hearts, we must also bring the sacrifices of "a broken spirit, a broken and contrite heart" (v. 17). God has to break us before he can make us. We have to allow his Spirit to break our stubborn wills, our pride, our attachment to sin.

With a cleansed heart and the Spirit within, David is now able to pray, "Then I will teach transgressors your ways, and sinners will turn back to you" (v. 13). When we become clean vessels, then God can use us. Only as we truly know him can we make him truly known.

There are many calls to vocation. Some are called to medicine, some to teaching, some to music, some to art, some to writing, some to the ministry. Men and women are called to these vocations by the aptitudes with which they are endowed. But the call to be holy is a call not to vocation but to character, and this call comes to everyone. We are each called to a life of holiness, a lifelong process by which our hearts and minds are conformed to Christ.

Dr. Lloyd Ogilvie, Chaplain of the U.S. Senate, once shared with me in an interview that on the wall of his office in Washington is a statement made by William Booth, founder of The Salvation Army. Booth, when once asked the secret of his success, replied, "I gave to God all there was of William Booth, and never took it back." Ogilvie said he keeps that statement before him as a reminder that God each day should have all there is of Lloyd Ogilvie. Only when David surrendered all there was of him to God did he experience the Spirit's transforming work in his life.

Psalm 51 is a call and a prayer for wholeness and holiness of heart and life. "This is the most deeply affecting of all the Psalms," confessed the saintly Thomas Chalmers, "and I am sure the one most applicable to me." Psalm 51 is the spiritual biography of every believer. God would lead each of us from pollution to pardon, to purity, and to power for service.

Hallelujah, God can make a saint out of a sinner!

Lord, lead me to wholeness. Fill my whole being with your presence and power and praise.

CHAPTER 53

From Fear to Faith

PSALM 55

> *Cast your cares on the* LORD
> *and he will sustain you.*
> (55:22)

THE PSALMIST IS SUFFERING a season of deep distress. He pleads with God to hear his supplication (v. 1). He is restless (v. 2), oppressed by enemies (v. 3), and besieged by the terrors of death (v. 4). Some scholars believe that this psalm was written on the occasion of the rebellion and treachery of Absalom, which for David was the apex of his sorrows.

Many of David's immortal psalms were forged in the crucible of affliction. "No man ever described a wounded heart like David," observed Adam Clarke. Distress and fear of "the terrors of death" are common to human beings. The psalmist elsewhere reminds us that there are no pockets in the shroud of death: "For he will take nothing with him when he dies, his splendor will not descend with him" (49:17).

Like David, we too may have expressed the wish, "Oh, that I had the wings of a dove! I would fly away and be at rest" (v. 6). The dove saves itself by its speed of flight and finds secure hiding places in the rock. Like David, we too may desire the security and serenity of the dove. But we cannot flee life's adversities. We are earthbound creatures for whom there is no escape from the reality of challenge and crisis.

Psychologists tell us that we are programmed to the instinctive reactions to danger of fight or flight. In "fight," the pulse quickens, the adrenalin flows, and we are endowed with increased strength. In "flight," we seek to escape the danger, sometimes by denial, withdrawal, or passive-aggressive behavior such as silence.

In our spiritual combat, if we resort to "flight" and run away from trouble, our fears and foes will only follow us. Nor can we on our own overcome by "fight." The issues and contests of life are greater than our strength alone.

But we can overcome by faith. The psalmist found the answer in his trust in God as exercised in his prayer life: "Evening and morning and at noon I will pray" (v. 17, NKJV). When the outlook is not good, we need to take the "uplook." God will make the difference.

By faith and the power of the Holy Spirit we become "more than conquerors" of the worst that life can throw at us. Even death loses its terror, as witnessed in the dying words of John Wesley, "The best of all is, God is with us!"

Joshua Liebman, in his book titled *Peace of Mind,* tells of an experience he had as a young man. He made a list of the supreme gifts in life and took them to a wise mentor. When he showed him the list he expected to be praised for his precocity. The list included health, love, talent, riches, beauty. As he shared the list with the wise old man, the sage got a twinkle in his eye. He reached for a pencil and carefully scratched through all of the things young Liebman had listed. Then the old man said, "You may have all of these, but they will turn out to be enemies instead of friends unless you have the one thing you missed." Then he wrote on the paper: "The gift of an untroubled mind." The psalmist gives us the secret for finding this great gift of an untroubled mind: "Cast your cares on the LORD and he will sustain you" (v. 22). The word "cast" suggests release, surrender of life's burdens and those things that would trouble us.

The pinnacle of the psalmist's faith is expressed in the radiant and ringing truth proclaimed in the concluding words of his song. This verse inspired Albert Orsborn to write the chorus that can be the testimony of every believer:

> *I have cast my burden on the Savior,*
>   *And while I pray,*
> *I shall find in Jesus all the help I need*
>   *On the upward way.*
> *It is not in sorrow to defeat me,*
>   *Nor the cheering ray of hope to dim,*
> *For the present shows God's mercy,*
>   *And the future is with him.*

Divine Helper, I cast my cares upon you in the assurance that you will sustain me.

CHAPTER 54

A Cornucopia of Blessing

PSALM 66

> *Come and see what God has done,*
> *how awesome his works in man's behalf!*
> (66:5)

SCIENCE HAS NEVER REVEALED half of what God in his goodness does to fertilize the earth and make it fruitful. Luther calls God the "Master-Cultivator who does everything to make it prosper." In the preceding Psalm 65, the psalmist, perhaps at a time of harvest festival, praises God for his providence, exclaiming in exalted speech:

> *You care for the land and water it;*
>   *you enrich it abundantly . . .*
> *you soften it with showers*
>   *and bless its crops.*
> *You crown the year with your bounty . . .*
>   *the hills are clothed with gladness . . .*
>   *and the valleys are mantled with grain;*
>   *they shout for joy and sing.*

> (65:9-13)

The goodness of God is manifest in all of nature, but perhaps no more so than in the marvelous provision of water. The giant ocean reservoirs are salted for purity, and into them are poured the waters of all the rivers. Then, by the process of evaporation, the land is supplied and refreshed with water falling from the clouds. The providence of nature proclaims both a mighty and a merciful God.

Psalm 66 begins with a paean of praise to God for his creation. The world becomes a hymn to the Eternal:

> *Shout with joy to God, all the earth!*
> *Sing to the glory of his name;*
> *offer him glory and praise!*
> *Say to God, "How awesome are your deeds!"* (vv. 1-2)

All human honors and works are trivial, mere dust on the pages of history. Although David, the author of this psalm, had notable achievements, he does not speak of what he has done but instead invites others to "Come and see what God has done, how awesome his works in man's behalf!"

He goes on to invite his audience to "come and hear . . . and I will declare what He has done for my soul" (v. 16, NKJV). He testifies, "God has surely listened and heard my voice in prayer" (v. 19). God is praised not only for his glory but also for his grace, not only for his creation of the world but also for his creative work within our lives. We, like the psalmist, praise God for his answer to prayer and for all that he has done for our souls.

But in the midst of his praise, the psalmist gives a caveat: "If I had cherished sin in my heart, the Lord would not have listened" (v. 18). Sin hinders prayer. God hears and answers prayer only when we come to him with pure motive and a clean heart. Then, with the psalmist, we will be able to say, "God has not rejected my prayer or withheld his love from me."

The Lord looks not at the eloquence of our prayers, to see

how articulate they are; nor at the geometry of our prayers, to see how long they are; nor at the arithmetic of our prayers, to see how many they are; nor at the logic of our prayers, to see how clever they are. But he looks at the sincerity of our prayers, to see how authentic they are.

The psalmist's prayer issues forth into praise (vv. 19-20). We too have received a cornucopia of blessings, a boundless benevolence from the bounty of God. We too have received his blessing in answered prayer for the deep needs of our souls. Let us then heed the advice of Matthew Henry: "What we win by prayer, we must wear with praise."

Lord of the harvest, give me a heart of praise for the bounty of your providence.

CHAPTER 55

The Hope of Old Age

PSALM 71

> *Even when I am old and gray,*
> *do not forsake me, O God.*
> (71:18)

"YOUTH WELL SPENT," SAID Seneca, "is the greatest comfort of old age." Our psalmist testifies to the serenity that comes from a long life of trust in God. This psalm portrays one, now advanced in years, who looks back in grateful remembrance of God's faithfulness. "For you have been my hope, O Sovereign LORD," he affirms, "my confidence since my youth" (v. 5).

"I have become as a wonder to many" (v. 7, NKJV), he exclaims. God's faithful people are viewed with wonderment. They are different from the world. They manifest a peace, poise, and power that are unworldly. Each believer's life shows forth the wonder-working power of God and his grace.

"Do not cast me away when I am old; do not forsake me when my strength is gone" (v. 9), the psalmist prays. His concern about his advancing years is such that he repeats his petition. "Even when I am old and gray, do not forsake me, O God" (v. 18). *The Message* paraphrases this verse: "But don't turn me out to pasture when I'm old or put me on the shelf when I can't pull my weight." Many dread old age and its infirmities, which Shakespeare described as "mere oblivion,/Sans teeth, sans eyes, sans taste, sans everything."

Another has described the passing years as follows:

> *When as a babe I smiled and wept – time slept;*
> *When as a child I laughed and leapt – time crept;*
> *When as a youth I dreamed and talked – time walked;*
> *Then I became a full grown man – time ran;*
> *As older still I daily grew – time flew;*
> *Soon I shall find in traveling on – time gone;*
> *O Christ, wilt thou have saved me then? – Amen!*

The toll of the years claims our strength and youthful beauty, but it does not take the blessing of God's presence and peace. With his own strength waning, the psalmist affirms: "I will go in the strength of the Lord GOD" (v. 16, NKJV). It would be frightening to face the infirmities of declining years apart from the assurance of God's love and care. He has given a precious promise just for old age: "Even to your old age and gray hairs I am he, I am he who will sustain you" (Isa. 46:4).

The ringing assurance of the aged psalmist is this: "But as for me, I will always have hope; I will praise you more and more" (v. 14). Elsewhere the psalmist tells us that the righteous "still bear fruit in old age" (92:14). Tennyson at age 83 wrote his *Crossing the Bar,* with its confident outlook:

> *I hope to see my Pilot face to face*
> *When I have crossed the bar.*

At 83 John Wesley was annoyed because he could not write more than 15 hours a day without hurting his eyes; at 86 he was ashamed that he could not preach more than twice a day. We are as old as our doubt, but as young as our faith.

Age makes things around us decay, but age makes the Christian flourish. The work of the vintage psalmist – and of God's followers – on earth is not yet done, for he aspires to "declare your power to the next generation, your might to all who are to come" (v. 18). The greatest legacy we can leave to the next generation is our faith and trust in God.

Eternal God, help me not to "go old," but to "grow old," buoyed by the assurance of your precious promise.

CHAPTER 56

The Beatitude of Worship

PSALM 84

> *Blessed are those who dwell in your house.*
> (84:4)

THE WARM DEVOTION AND lyrical cadence of Psalm 84 have found eloquent expression in the well-known setting of Brahms' classic *German Requiem*. The psalm expresses the deep longing of the heart for the place and presence of God. It easily divides into three sections of four verses, each with its own beatitude that summarizes the blessing of its joyful theme.

First, there is the beatitude of worship: "Blessed are those who dwell in your house; they are ever praising you" (v. 4). The psalmist longs for the tabernacle of God, not for its own sake, but for the sake of God's presence found there. It has been said that memory was given us that we might have summer's roses in wintertime. The psalmist remembers the fragrance of God's presence in the tabernacle and cries out:

> *How lovely is your dwelling place,*
>   *O LORD Almighty!*
> *My soul yearns, even faints*
>   *for the courts of the LORD;*
> *My heart and my flesh cry out*
>   *for the living God.*
>
> (vv. 1-2)

The temple was a place for realizing God's presence and worshiping him. C. H. Spurgeon describes the psalmist's plea: "He wept, he sighed, he pleaded for the privilege. He needed no clatter of bells from the belfry to ring him in; he carried his bell in his own bosom. Holy appetite is a better call to worship than a full chime."

It is believed that this psalm was written by David either when he was fleeing Saul or during the rebellion of Absalom. In each instance he was isolated from worship in the tabernacle. There are many today, in lands where religious freedom is not enjoyed and Christians are persecuted for their faith, who long for the courts of God. They are denied the opportunity of corporate worship in accordance with their faith.

Dietrich Bonhoeffer, separated from the fellowship of the church that had so nourished his life, wrote to his parents from prison: "Well, Whitsuntide is here, and we are still separated. When the bells rang this morning, I longed to go to church." For many, often the most sacred things of life are not truly appreciated until they are lost.

The Salvation Army has not been without its heroes and heroines of the faith. The movement was born in sacrifice and persecution. Its pioneers suffered great opposition and violence. William Booth, its founder, said, "It's our troubles that give us our anecdotes." Those familiar with the history of the movement will call to mind stalwarts within the ranks who paid a high cost for fidelity to Christ. Major Yin Hung-shun endured fifteen years in a labor camp in China. Brigadier Josef Korbel was imprisoned for over ten years in Czechoslovakia. Major Noh Young Soo was executed by the communists in Korea. Two young women teachers were murdered by terrorists at an Army compound in Zimbabwe in 1978. These, with many others, grace the Army's Roll of Heroes.

Many throughout history have known the poignancy of the psalmist's cry for the courts of God. Their stories should remind us of the sacred privilege of corporate worship in places set aside for that purpose.

Let us, who enjoy the privilege of freedom of worship, love the house of the Lord as the psalmist did. Let us know, as expressed in this beatitude, the blessedness of those who "dwell" in God's house. Let us be found there with those who praise the Lord.

Sovereign God, give me a heart yearning for your presence and worship.

CHAPTER 57

The Beatitude of Strength

PSALM 84, CONTINUED

> *Blessed are those whose strength is in you.*
> (84:5)

THE SECOND BEATITUDE of Psalm 84 rejoices in the strength we receive from the Lord: "Blessed are those whose strength is in you, who have set their hearts on pilgrimage" (v. 5). The psalmist here refers to those making their spiritual pilgrimage:

"as they pass through the Valley of Baca, they make it a place of springs; the autumn rains also cover it with pools."

Baca means "weeping"; thus the valley of Baca is a valley of tears. But God's people turn barrenness into blessedness, making a well from which will be drawn waters of refreshment and sustenance. If we are unable to create a well of water from below, then the rain will come from above to sustain us.

We note that the text reads, "As they pass through." Trouble is not a dead-end path. God leads us through it. A certain Christian was known for always saying in testimony meetings that she was blessed by the words "and it came to pass." She added, "When trouble comes, I bless the Lord it didn't come to stay – it came to pass!"

Fanny Crosby became blind soon after birth. But she "dug a well in the valley of Baca" and gave the world songs of praise that have cheered multitudes of Christians on their pilgrimage from earth to heaven. In that valley, she found a well that not only quenched her thirst but overflowed to bring refreshment to a great multitude. One of her much-loved songs from that well is this:

> A Wonderful Savior is Jesus, my Lord,
> A Wonderful Savior to me;
> He hideth my soul in the cleft of the rock,
> Where rivers of pleasure I see.

Myra Brooks Welch, a noted poet, penned her masterpiece, "The Touch of the Master's Hand," from a wheelchair. On one occasion she pointed to the wheelchair and said, "I thank God for this," for her talent had lain undiscovered until she was confined to it. She "dug a well in the valley of Baca," and from it many have slaked their spiritual thirst.

Such persons "go from strength to strength" (v. 7). On our spiritual pilgrimage, when we are in the company of the Lord, nourished by his presence and the Spirit's power, we grow stronger each day.

The third and final beatitude of this psalm is: "Blessed is the man who trusts in you." The words of Thomas Kelly express the blessedness of trust for every believer:

> *When we cannot see our way,*
> *Let us trust and still obey;*
> *He who bids us forward go,*
> *Cannot fail the way to show.*
>
> *Though it be the gloom of night,*
> *Though we see no ray of light,*
> *Since the Lord himself is there,*
> *'Tis not meet that we should fear.*
>
> *Be it ours, then, while we're here,*
> *Him to follow without fear,*
> *Where He calls us, there to go,*
> *What He bids us, that to do.*

Almighty God, enable me by prayer and faith to go from strength to strength.

CHAPTER 58

Doorkeepers

PSALM 84, CONTINUED

> *I would rather be a doorkeeper in the house of my God*
> *Than dwell in the tents of wickedness.*
> (84:10, NKJV)

MANY GO TO CHURCH early in life just to satisfy a parent's wish or requirement. But later, when they come to know the salvation of Christ and the indwelling of the Holy Spirit, their attitude changes: some of their most blessed hours are spent in God's presence and in the company of his people. With the psalmist they would say: "Better is one day in your courts than a thousand elsewhere" (v. 10).

There is an old saying, "If I had my druthers," meaning if I had my choice. The psalmist, expressing his "druthers," says: "I would rather be a doorkeeper in the house of my God than dwell in the tents of wickedness."

C. H. Spurgeon writes on this text: "God's worst is better than the devil's best. God's doorstep is a happier rest than downy couches within the pavilions of royal sinners, though we might lie there for a lifetime of luxury."

Doorkeepers fulfill an important function in the house of the Lord. They are the first ones in and the last ones out, seeing the worshipers safely on their way. They also have the sacred function and high privilege of ushering others over the threshold to the One who said, "I am the door." In this sense, we are all called to be doorkeepers in the house of the Lord, encouraging and helping others to come into our Father's home.

A famous story is told of St. Francis: one day he said to one of his young friars, "Let us go down to the village and preach to the people." So they went, with the young man eager to observe the preaching of his saintly mentor. On the way they stopped to talk to this man and to that. Francis stopped to play with the children, exchanged greetings with passers-by, and spoke comfortingly to those who were suffering. Then they turned to go home. "But father," said the novice, "when do we preach?" "Preach?" smiled Francis. "Every step we took, every word we spoke, every action we did, has been a sermon."

Sometimes the doorkeeper in the Lord's house, by a friendly smile, a warm handshake, and a genuine "God bless you," may preach a more effective sermon than the preacher on a given day. No service rendered to God is menial; rather, in the Lord's hands our modest offerings of loaves and fishes become multiplied blessings in the lives of others.

Brother Lawrence (1611-1691) bequeathed to us his classic memoir of the devotional life, *The Practice of the Presence of God*. He referred to himself as "the lord of all pots and pans" in honor of his employment in the kitchen of the monastery until his death at the age of 80. For him no task was too trivial, as he transformed the mundane chores of the kitchen into "the sacrament of the present moment."

The decision the psalmist faced is one that confronts every person. Each individual has to choose between "the house of the Lord" and "the tents of the wicked," between the holy and the secular, between God and the world.

George Beverly Shea had to make a choice as a young man – between pursuing a lucrative secular career as a singer or becoming a low-paid gospel soloist for Billy Graham's evangelistic crusades. His decision resulted in his becoming the best-known gospel singer in all of history, spending over half a century reaching millions of souls in a worldwide ministry. He put into music his testimony of that decision:

> I'd rather have Jesus than silver or gold,
>   I'd rather be his than have riches untold;
> I'd rather have Jesus than houses or lands,
>   I'd rather be led by his nail-pierced hand.
>
> I'd rather have Jesus than men's applause,
>   I'd rather be faithful to his dear cause;
> I'd rather have Jesus than worldwide fame,
>   I'd rather be true to his holy name.

(1939; words by Rhea F. Miller)

Heavenly Father, may I ever choose the eternal over the earthly, the true treasures of life over this world's tinsel.

CHAPTER 59

A Golden Promise

PSALM 84, CONTINUED

> *For the LORD God is a sun and shield.*
> (84:11)

PSALM 84, CALLED A "jewel among the psalms," concludes with a radiant and golden promise:

> *For the LORD God is a sun and shield;*
> *the LORD bestows favor and honor;*
> *no good thing does he withhold*
> *from those whose walk is blameless.*

> (v. 11)

The Lord is to us a sun. He is our source of light, of beauty, of life. He floods our prosaic paths with his divine radiance. He guides us through the dark and difficult places.

To one who asked, "Give me a light that I may tread safely into the unknown," came the reply: "Go out into the darkness and put your hand into the hand of God. That shall be to you better than a light and safer than a known way."

The story is told that the famed Scottish hero Robert Bruce, when fleeing his enemies, took refuge in a cave and there prayed for God's protection. A spider wove a web across the cave's entrance. His pursuers came to the cave, but, seeing the spider web across its opening, thought he could not have en-

tered without breaking the web and went on their way. Later
Bruce said, "Without God, a stone wall is as a spider web; with
God a spider web is as a stone wall."

The Lord is to us a shield. We are engaged in a life-and-
death struggle. There is no demilitarized zone for the Christian. No war is fought with greater fierceness than the spiritual combat in which we find ourselves. Foes are both without
and within. We need a shield to save us from the fierce assaults
of Satan, and we need strength to control passions, to subdue
appetites, and to repulse the inclinations of self-will. Alone,
we are inadequate and would be defeated. But the Lord our
Shield will protect and strengthen us and enable us to be victorious.

No good thing will he withhold from those who faithfully
do his will. God does not promise to satisfy all our wants and desires. He will, however, give to us his grace, his peace, his joy, his
power – and above all himself. "The LORD will give grace and
glory" (v. 11, NKJV) is a promise that represents the sum of all
God's blessing to humankind. But we cannot have this glory
without first experiencing God's grace. This golden promise is
for those who have put their trust in God.

In the words of Robert Grant, we sing of the Lord as our
Shield, and of his might and grace:

> O worship the King, all glorious above;
>   O gratefully sing his power and his love;
> Our shield and defender, the Ancient of Days,
>   Pavilioned in splendor and girded with praise.
>
> O tell of his might, O sing of his grace,
>   Whose robe is the light, whose canopy space;

His chariots of wrath the deep thunderclouds form,
  And dark is his path on the wings of the storm.

Frail children of dust and feeble as frail,
  In thee do we trust, nor find thee to fail;
Thy mercies how tender, how firm to the end,
  Our Maker, Defender, Redeemer and Friend.

(1833)

Divine Spendthrift on my behalf, I praise you for your good gifts of glory and grace so lavishly bestowed.

CHAPTER 60

The Eternity of God

PSALM 90

> Lord, you have been our dwelling place
> throughout all generations.
> (90:1)

THE LOFTY THEOLOGY AND theme of this psalm are nothing less than God's eternity and human transience. The ascription identifies it as a "prayer of Moses the man of God." Thus it is invested with the experience and faith of one of the spiritual giants of the Bible, the one to whom God spoke "as a man to his friend." This is the oldest composition in the Psalter, but its eloquently expressed truths are timeless.

Moses did not write these words from the palace of Pharaoh, but from the barren wilderness through which he wandered with the Israelites for forty years, during which 600,000 Israelites died for their unbelief, a stark reminder of their mortality. He, with his people, had no dwelling place on earth, only a moving tent as they pressed on. They could not plant a garden, they could not plan and build a home, they could not become attached to a place and settle down. They had to be always journeying, always traveling, ever moving onward from place to place, never settled.

They could never feel secure, for they were pilgrims going through a land where they were unwanted. Each day exposed them to the dangers of their enemies, wild beasts, and pestilence. But as Moses, the man of God, contemplated their situation, he realized that though he and his people lived in tents, they had something better than an earthly abode: "Lord, you have been our dwelling place throughout all generations" (v. 1). In the eternal God they possessed blessing and security that no temporal home could afford.

Moses had turned over to God the key to his heart, the place where his faith and affection were centered. In the eternal God he found a home for himself and his people that would never change or pass away. The God who inhabits the heavens also deigns to dwell with us, to be our Helper, our Friend, our heavenly Father.

In answer to the question, "What is eternity?" someone replied, "It is the lifetime of the Almighty." The psalmist, in contemplating God, expresses the lofty thought: "Before the mountains were born . . . from everlasting to everlasting you are God" (v. 2). Mountains, those ancient giants, are but mere novelties of an hour in the vast eternity of God. Before all the countless galaxies and stars – God was! Our time is but as a millisecond to God's eternity: "For a thousand years in your sight are like a day that has just gone by" (v. 4).

It staggers the imagination to ponder that God is "from everlasting to everlasting." He had no beginning. Our finite minds cannot grasp such infinite dimensions. But then, if the finite could grasp the infinite, the infinite would be finite. We need a Creator who transcends the boundaries of our most daring imaginings. A. W. Tozer challenges us to discover the ravishing majesty of God: we "may live a full lifetime and die without once having our minds challenged by the sweet mystery of the Godhead. At the contemplation and utterance of his majesty, all eloquence is rightly dumb and all mental effort is feeble."

May we, with the psalmist, know the comforting assurance of having God as our dwelling place, for which he has given us an eternal lease. He is our rest and our refuge. In his safe keeping our hearts and hopes are centered. The Apostle John caught the wonder of this experience for us in Christ when he recorded: "We know that we live in him and he in us, because he has given us of his Spirit" (1 John 4:13). Let us find our rest in this dwelling place of the eternal God, our heritage throughout eternity.

Eternal God, keep me ever under the spell of your might and majesty, your grace and glory.

CHAPTER 61

The Mortality of Mankind

PSALM 90, CONTINUED

> *The length of our days . . . quickly pass.*
> (90:10)

THIS PSALM PREACHES HUMAN mortality in immortal words. It is only natural to go from contemplation of the eternity of God to thoughts of the mortality of mankind, expressed in perhaps the most frequently quoted verse of this psalm: "The length of our days is seventy years – or eighty, if we have the strength . . . they quickly pass, and we fly away" (v. 10).

Our frail and fleeting life all too quickly flies away from us. Its brevity has long been commented on in Scripture and by poets and philosophers. Job plaintively lamented: "Man born of woman is of few days and full of trouble. He springs up like a flower and withers away; like a fleeting shadow, he does not endure" (Job 14:1). James, in his short epistle, echoes the sentiment: "What is your life? You are a mist that appears for a little while and then vanishes" (James 4:14). Seneca observed: "The hour which gives us life begins to take it away." Shakespeare added his verdict in *Macbeth*:

> *Life's but a walking shadow, a poor player*
> *That struts and frets his hour upon the stage,*
> *And then is heard no more.*

Longfellow, in his *A Psalm of Life*, gave his haunting assessment:

Art is long, and Time is fleeting,
And our hearts, though stout and brave,
Still, like muffled drums, are beating
Funeral marches to the grave.

The psalmist cannot stop at his contemplation of the brevity of life. He has to come to a conclusion, to a plan of life and a course of action in light of this truth. His lesson is epitomized in verse 12, in the form of a prayer: "Teach us to number our days aright, that we may gain a heart of wisdom." Of all arithmetic exercises we may undertake, the hardest is this – to number our days. We can count our wealth, our possessions, material things around us, but how many of us can count our days, adding to those we have had the number we have left? Only the gravestones in cemeteries witness to the number of days.

Yet the psalmist prays, "Teach us to number our days aright." He is speaking, of course, to the quality more than to the quantity of our days of life. Thomas Fuller has reminded us: "He lives long that lives well; and time misspent is not lived, but lost." Another has prayed: "Teach me to live that I may dread the grave as little as my bed."

When we submit this transient life to God's eternity, our quickly passing days and years to his eternal purpose, then the closing prayer of this psalm will be fulfilled in us: "May the favor of the Lord our God rest upon us; establish the work of our hands for us" (v. 17).

Isaac Watts, inspired by this psalm, has enriched our hymnals with this paraphrase of its text:

O God, our help in ages past,
Our hope for years to come,

Our shelter from the stormy blast,
   And our eternal home.

Before the hills in order stood,
   Or earth received her frame,
From everlasting Thou art God,
   To endless years the same.

Time, like an ever-rolling stream,
   Bears all its sons away;
They fly forgotten, as a dream
   Dies at the opening day.

O God, our help in ages past,
   Our hope for years to come,
Be thou our guard while life shall last,
   And our eternal home.

(1719)

Eternal God, teach me to come to terms with both my mortality and your eternity.

CHAPTER 62

Dwelling in God

PSALM 91

> *He who dwells in the shelter of the Most High*
> *will rest in the shadow of the Almighty.*
> (91:1)

THIS NOBLE PSALM SPEAKS of the security of the believer.
But it is a conditional security. The condition is that we maintain close fellowship with God. We need to dwell in that inner
sanctuary of the presence of God, to reside habitually in his
presence.

Thomas Kelly, in his classic work, *A Testament of Devotion,*
writes with rare discernment on this theme: "Deep within us
all there is an amazing inner sanctuary of the soul, a holy
place, a Divine Center, a speaking Voice, to which we may con-
tinuously return. Eternity is at our hearts, pressing upon our
time-torn lives, warming us with intimations of an astounding destiny, calling us home unto Itself." It is this "astounding
destiny" and intimate fellowship with God to which Psalm 91
calls us.

A guide was taking tourists through a power plant in Niag-
ara Falls that harnessed power from the mighty volume of water to create electricity for the lighting of cities and homes, the
turning of factory wheels, the manufacturing of clothing and
processing of food. At the end of the tour, he took them into a
large room with many complex-looking machines. In that

room, there was not a person to be seen at work, nor any sound to be heard. "This is the still room," explained the guide. "This is the center of the whole thing; the whole process hinges on what is done here. It is the most important place in the building."

This story provides a parable of our lives. Wonderful power can flow from our lives out of the resources God has made available to us. But we must have a "still room," a secret place where God can accomplish his purpose in us. Amid our sound-soaked days and nights, our life needs a rhythm that includes stopping, solitude, and stillness. "Without solitude," writes Henry Nouwen, "it is virtually impossible to live a spiritual life."

The insightful Catholic monk Thomas Merton (1915-1968), in his autobiography, *Seven Storey Mountain,* and in many other writings, bridges the Eastern and Western world, the world of contemplation and the world of activism. He writes: "The world of men has forgotten the joys of silence, the peace of solitude which is necessary, to some extent, for the fullness of human living. If a man is locked out of his spiritual solitude he ceases to be a true person. Man becomes a kind of automaton, living without joy, because he has lost all spontaneity. He is no longer moved from within, but only from outside himself. Such a man no longer acts upon the outside world, but lets it act upon him."

Richard Foster, in his book *Prayer,* mentions that he has on occasion put a sign on his office door that those around him understand: "In Conference with the Boss." The maintenance of our spiritual life needs those times when we withdraw from the world around us, even from those closest to us, to be with God and replenish the resources of our soul.

We would make the words of John Greenleaf Whittier our prayer:

> *Dear Lord and Father of mankind,*
> *Forgive our foolish ways;*
> *Reclothe us in our rightful mind;*
> *In purer lives Thy service find*
> *In deeper reverence, praise.*
>
> *Drop Thy still dews of quietness*
> *Till all our strivings cease;*
> *Take from our souls the strain and stress,*
> *And let our ordered lives confess*
> *the beauty of Thy peace.*

(1872)

Help me, Lord, to know the sheltering place and shadow of your presence that will protect me in the heat of the day's journey.

CHAPTER 63

Secure in God

PSALM 91, CONTINUED

> *I will say of the LORD, "He is my refuge and my fortress,*
> *my God, in whom I trust."*
>
> (91:2)

LUTHER CALLED THIS PSALM "the most distinguished jewel among all the psalms of consolation." In it the poet assures us of God's everlasting vigil over his people.

The metaphors in this psalm are drawn from ancient nomadic life. "The fowler's snare" (v. 3) or bird-catcher's trap represents the traps Satan sets for us. He is still the arch deceiver. The cunning and craft of our adversary might well alarm us, except for the protective presence and power of God.

"He will cover you with his feathers, and under his wings you will find refuge" (v. 4). God is pictured poetically as a mother bird sheltering her chicks. The possible catastrophes listed here include "terror," "arrow," "pestilence," and "plague." The psalmist of the ancient world lived with the terror of history. Without warning, marauding armies or plagues could sweep upon him. Life is still a dangerous business, and we desperately need the protection of the Almighty.

Verses 11-12 have become well known as cited by Satan in the temptation of Jesus (Matthew 4:6). However, Satan left out a very important part of this text: "to guard you in all your ways." Satan, in his temptation, could not quote this part of the text.

"For he will command his angels concerning you to guard you in all your ways" (v. 11). This is thought by some to be a proof text for guardian angels. Angels are God's messengers to carry out his will among human beings. "Are not all angels ministering spirits sent to serve those who will inherit salvation?" (Hebrews 1:14).

"They will lift you up in their hands, so that you will not strike your foot against a stone" (v. 12). "Stone" may represent trivial and unexpected obstacles that can catch us off guard. The "lion" (v. 13) portrays Satan, fierce and active and out to "devour" the Christian. The "cobra" (v. 13) lurks silently in the most pleasant meadows to claim victims in the most unexpected ways. The "dragon" (v. 13, KJV) could represent imagined ills that become real because we think they are real.

Modern society intensely pursues security. We build and stockpile colossal weapons, even as we know that our great cities stand only by sufferance and could be destroyed in an hour. We invest enormous amounts of effort and money in medical research, only to be subject to more and more new diseases. World leaders make international treaties for security that are broken upon the slightest provocation. In God alone is security for the believer.

Being a Christian is not an insurance policy against dangers. Rather, it is the assurance that God will keep our souls inviolable for all eternity. Paul in prison, Dietrich Bonhoeffer going to the gallows, Corrie Ten Boom enduring the horrors of the Holocaust – such suffering does not contradict the promise of this psalm but rather puts it in true perspective. We are assured, "'Because he loves me,' says the LORD, 'I will rescue him'" (v. 14). When we trust in God, he will place us in the eye of the storm, with an inner serenity and stability amid the storm that surrounds us.

As C. S. Lewis observed, the Christian life consists of peaks and troughs. When we are on the peaks, it is important to remember that the troughs will come. And when we are in the troughs, we must not forget the peaks.

John Greenleaf Whittier caught the assurance of this psalm with these comforting lines from "The Eternal Goodness":

> *I know not where his islands lift*
> *Their fronded palms in air;*
> *I only know I cannot drift*
> *Beyond his love and care.*

Great God, life is a dangerous journey. Keep me from evil by your presence and power.

CHAPTER 64

Come with Singing

Psalm 95

> *Come, let us sing for joy to the Lord.*
> (95:1)

THE PSALMIST HERE INVITES us to some of the most noble and lofty exercises of the soul. Five times his invitation rings out, "Let us . . . ":

Come, let us sing for joy to the LORD;
  let us shout aloud to the Rock of our salvation.

(v. 1)

Let us come before him with thanksgiving.

(v. 2)

Come, let us bow down in worship,
  let us kneel before the LORD our Maker.

(v. 6)

The word "come" intensifies the personal invitation of the psalmist. This is no routine invitation; rather, it is a summons to the soul for an audience with the Creator of the world. It is an invitation that must take precedence over all other engagements of life.

And how does one come into such an august presence? With fear and trembling? With servile submission out of respect for his divinity? His power could warrant such an approach. But that is not what the psalmist says. Rather, the invitation is to come into his presence singing.

Every Christian should have an intimate acquaintance with two books: the Bible and the hymn book. Ours is a faith that issues forth in songs of praise and devotion. With Isaac Watts, we are constrained to praise in song:

Begin, my tongue, some heavenly theme
  And speak some boundless thing;
The mighty works or mightier name
  Of our eternal King.

Tell of his wondrous faithfulness
    And sound his power abroad;
Sing the sweet promise of his grace,
    The love and truth of God.

(1707)

Our songs to our Creator are in the major key, joyful and ju-bilant. The psalmist is not referring to a superficial expression of joy, a mere emotional sequence and outburst of musical notes. God deserves and requires that our expressions be thoughtful and reverent as well as joyful.

In his *Reflections on the Psalms,* C. S. Lewis writes of the note of praise resonating in the psalms:

> I want to stress what I think that we (or at least I) need more; the joy and delight in God which meet us in the Psalms. . . . These poets knew far less reason than we for lov-ing God. They did not know that He offered them eternal joy; still less that He would die to win it for them. Yet they express a longing for Him, for His mere presence, which comes only to the best Christians or to Christians in their best moments. . . . They are glad and rejoice. Their fingers itch for the harp, for the lute and the harp. . . . Let's have a song, bring the tambourine, bring the 'merry harp with the lute,' we're going to sing merrily and make a cheerful noise. . . . Let us have the clashing cymbals, not only well tuned, but *loud,* and dances too.

Lewis further observes that other traditions, including the Roman Catholic Church and The Salvation Army, "have re-tained more of it than we [Anglicans]. We have a terrible concern about good taste." May none of us forfeit that joyful spontaneity to which the psalmist invites us, and which so impressed this eminent Christian scholar.

Thank you, God, for inviting me to a joyful and jubilant manner of worship.

CHAPTER 65

Come with Thanksgiving

PSALM 95, CONTINUED

> Let us come before him with thanksgiving
> and extol him with music and song.
> (95:2)

WE CANNOT COME INTO the presence of God without a keen awareness of his bountiful blessings. How unspeakably good God has been to us. Therefore, "Let us come before him with thanksgiving."

Sometimes we do not thank enough because we do not think enough. When we truly consider what God has done for us, an irrepressible gratitude bursts forth.

The Psalms are soaked with the language of thanksgiving. It is hard to find a page in the Psalter that does not reverberate with thanksgiving. Thanksgiving spills over on top of thanksgiving as the psalmist exclaims, "O LORD my God, I will give you thanks forever" (30:12).

Worship is the culmination, the all-embracing act in our coming to God. It includes singing, joy, thanksgiving, adoration. It is the elevation of the soul in adoration and praise before the God of the universe. There is no higher exercise of our lives than to worship God.

In his book *Purity of Heart Is to Will One Thing,* the Danish philosopher-theologian Søren Kierkegaard spoke of worship as a drama. He insisted that in true worship the congregation are the actors, the ministers and choir are "prompters," and God is the audience. It is indeed an awesome thought that the God of the universe is attentive to our worship. It invests our worship experience with incalculable value and nobility.

The psalmist rejoices because we worship a God who is not only transcendent, enthroned afar in the universe, but also the One who is "our God and we are the people of his pasture, the flock under his care" (v. 7). We come to the One who is our Shepherd, who lovingly cares for us and gave his Son to die for us that we might be forgiven and live with him forever.

Nearly a century ago, Henry van Dyke captured well the jubilant note of praise and worship:

> *Joyful, joyful, we adore thee,*
>   *God of glory, Lord of love;*
> *Hearts unfold like flowers before thee,*
>   *Opening to the sun above.*
> *Melt the clouds of sin and sadness,*
>   *Drive the dark of doubt away;*
> *Giver of immortal gladness,*
>   *Fill us with the light of day.*

All thy works with joy surround thee,
Earth and heaven reflect thy rays,
Stars and angels sing around thee,
Center of unbroken praise;
Field and forest, vale and mountain,
Flowery meadow, flashing sea,
Chanting bird and flowing fountain
Call us to rejoice in thee.

(1907)

The psalmist proceeds from the theme of worship (vv. 1-7a) to that of warning (7b-11). "Today" – God never allows for procrastination. His call is urgent, immediate. Our eternal destiny is at stake. "If" – what a dreadful possibility it is that we may elect not to hear his voice. A fateful and fatal hardening of the heart takes place when we continue to ignore his call and compassion (v. 8). As with those who rebelled in the wilderness, so the one today who rejects God will not enter into his rest (vv. 9-11).

Let us indeed come to the Lord with thanksgiving, for we stand in the midst of riches that no money can buy. All around us the bounty and providence of God shower blessings without number. In the realm of God's care for us, the best things in life are free.

God of the universe, I am constrained to come into your presence with praise and thanksgiving.

CHAPTER 66

Reason to Sing

PSALM 96

> *Sing to the LORD, praise his name.*
> (96:2)

THE INSPIRING HISTORY OF this psalm is recorded in 1 Chronicles 16: "That day David first committed to Asaph and his associates this psalm of thanks to the LORD" (v. 7). Then follows much of the text of Psalms 10 and 96. What was "that day" to which the Chronicler refers? It was the day when David brought the Ark of the Covenant back to Jerusalem and to the tent erected for it.

The Ark of the Covenant was the most sacred treasure of Israel, symbolizing the mystical presence of God among his people. It was the most important part of the tabernacle worship while Israel traveled for forty years in the wilderness, before they took possession of the Promised Land. In it reposed the two tablets of stone engraved with the Ten Commandments.

It was a special box, overlaid with gold, the dimensions and design having been minutely detailed to Moses by God. It had a covering of pure gold, and the forms of two angels faced each other and looked down on the covering. The covering or lid was called the mercy seat, and the high priest placed the Old Testament offerings for the people upon it. God promised to commune with them from above the mercy seat.

The return of this sacred treasure to its spiritual home in Jerusalem was an occasion of irrepressible joy. It called for a new song. It seems David wrote the psalms to be sung and gave them to Asaph, his chief musician, to compose the music.

Modern Asaphs are still inspired to set the sublime beauty of psalms to music. I was privileged to be present where this was happening on one occasion. My son-in-law, Dr. Harold Burgmayer, a music director and composer, had sequestered himself in our mountain cabin retreat and was doing the final work on his composition of a selection for Salvation Army bands, based on this psalm, using the modern sound of the trumpet and other instruments of praise and devotion. The Christian community owes a great debt of gratitude to all such modern Asaphs who have set the inspired truths of the Psalms to music, so that we, like the psalmist and worshipers of old, may tune our spirits to their lofty themes of devotion.

What does all this mean to us in the twenty-first century? The Ark of the Covenant seems remote from our lives and faith. But a careful and literal rendering of John 1:14 from the Greek New Testament reads: "And the Word became flesh and tabernacled among us." The Ark is a symbol of Christ, the ultimate presence of God among human beings, the One whose name is Immanuel, meaning "God with us."

The return of Israel's most sacred treasure, the Ark, was the cause for a new song and great rejoicing. So too is the coming of Christ to our lives. He who is our most sacred treasure and the source of all our blessings is cause for a new song and our uninhibited praise.

Immanuel, I rejoice and sing a new song because you came to dwell in my life.

CHAPTER 67

A New Song

PSALM 96, CONTINUED

> *Sing to the LORD a new song.*
> (96:1)

THREE TIMES IN ITS first two verses this psalm invites us to sing:

> *Sing to the LORD a new song;*
> *sing to the LORD, all the earth.*
> *Sing to the LORD, praise his name.*
>
> (vv. 1-2)

Sing, sing, sing – three times the divine imperative sounds forth. The ability to sing is one of the gifts with which God has endowed humankind. The psalmist tells us that this gift is to be rendered to God – "Sing to the LORD." But what shall we sing?

With Tennyson in his *In Memoriam* we say, "I do but sing because I must." What God does for every life is cause for our individual *Te Deum*s. In each heart he has put a song of praise and thanksgiving. We are to sing a new song, for God is continuing to do new and wonderful things for us.

"Give me the making of the songs of a nation, and I care not who makes its laws," wrote Andrew Fletcher. We might paraphrase, "Give me the making of the songs of the church, and I care not who writes its theology." Do not the youth, as well as many adults of the church, often learn more theology from songs than from the most carefully formulated doctrinal statements? Theology is effectively conveyed – for good or ill, depending upon the quality of the music and its message – in the songs and music of our faith.

Psalm 96 is a song full of theological truths that inspire us to praise and devotion. It speaks to us of the unbridled joy that bursts into song when the presence of God comes into our lives. The Ark of the Covenant was an Old Testament symbol of God's presence among his people, ultimately to be known in and through Christ. When Christ comes to us – he who is the very presence of God, dwelling, not in a symbolic ark or tent, but within the sacred abode of our hearts – then we cannot restrain our joy. It bursts forth in the new song he puts in the heart.

On numerous occasions in the Bible, new songs were composed, inspired by what God had done. Moses recorded a song after the miraculous passage through the Red Sea (Exodus 15). Deborah and Barak wrote a song of triumph after the defeat of Sisera (Judges 5). Hannah wrote her beautiful hymn after the birth of Samuel (1 Samuel 2). Associated with the Advent are the songs of Mary, Zechariah, and Simeon.

Prophesying the coming ministry of Christ, Isaiah enjoins us to "Sing to the LORD a new song" (42:10). Referring to his deliverance by God, David testifies, "He put a new song in my mouth" (Psalm 40:3). In the last book of the Bible, John looks through his telescope of faith and describes the redeemed before the throne of God: "They sang a new song" (Revelation 5:9). Praise God, for he not only gives us a new song here in this life, but he will also give us a brand-new song, fashioned for the hearts and lips of his redeemed, to sing before his celestial throne.

And what shall the redeemed sing in that fair land? It will be a song of praise and adoration, for the redemption we have through his sacrifice, the universality of his kingdom, and our reigning with him forever (Revelation 5:9-10). What a theme for a song! No wonder there will be singing of a new song in heaven! Let us be sure to be there to join in that glorious anthem!

Eternal God, my song I raise in grateful overflowing praise.

CHAPTER 68

A Missionary Mandate

PSALM 96, CONTINUED

> *Declare his glory among the nations.*
> (96:3)

"DECLARE HIS GLORY AMONG the nations, his marvelous deeds among all peoples." This verse has been called "a missionary mandate of the Old Testament." It calls all nations to praise the Lord and to proclaim his glory throughout the world. It anticipates the world mission of the New Testament people of God.

The psalmist speaks with a felicitous phrase that is centuries ahead of his time: "families of nations" (v. 7). When Eva Burrows was international leader of The Salvation Army, she said of the one hundred or so countries in which the Army was active, "We are not a federation of nations, but a family of nations." Bramwell Booth, an earlier leader of the movement, had said to his troops, "All nations are my fatherland because all nations are my Father's land." When Salvationists of all races, colors, nationalities, and languages would gather for international events, there was a unity in their diversity that would make the United Nations blush with envy. Their bonding was in the love and salvation of Christ. His call to them and to us is: "Ascribe to the LORD, O families of nations, ascribe to the LORD glory and strength" (v. 7).

This psalm is still a commission to Christians to take the good tidings of the gospel to all peoples. Ours is a global gospel. Jesus himself gives the commission: "Therefore go and make disciples of all nations" (Matthew 28:19). Hundreds of millions have never heard of the Lord of glory. May we each do our part by prayer and stewardship to help all "families of nations" know the love and grace of their heavenly Father.

A little girl greeted her father one evening with the request, "Daddy, will you buy me a world?" The girl was of course referring to a globe. The father secured the globe and presented it to his little girl, who then said, "Oh, Daddy, I wanted a lighted world." Then she thought for a moment and said, "But I suppose a lighted world costs more." Children of God need to be willing to bear the costliness of making our world a lighted one instead of a darkened one in places where the Christian gospel has yet to be proclaimed.

"For great is the LORD" (v. 4). He is the God of unimaginable glory, of infinite splendor, of incomputable wonder! He is the God of "splendor and majesty . . . strength and glory" (v. 6).

Three times, after the greatness and glory of God are declared, we are enjoined to "give unto the LORD" (vv. 7-8, KJV). What could we bring to the Lord of the universe? We are such paupers before the God of the cosmos. Just think, there is something God wants from us!

God invites us to bring to him our praise (vv. 7-8) and our worship: "Worship the LORD in the splendor of his holiness" (v. 9). We are to come before him with cleansed hearts and purified motives so that we may worship him in spirit and truth. Then shall we be commissioned as his evangelists, to "show forth his salvation from day to day" (v. 2, JKV).

In culmination, all the universe joins in the harmony of praise and worship, even all inanimate creation rejoices because "The LORD reigns" (v. 10) and "he comes" (v. 13).

> Let the heavens rejoice, let the earth be glad;
>> let the sea resound, and all that is in it;
>> let the fields be jubilant, and everything in them.
> Then all the trees of the forest will sing for joy;
>> they will sing before the LORD, for he comes.

(vv. 11-13)

May our response be the same as those who long ago first rejoiced in the singing of this psalm, of whom the Chronicler wrote: "Then all the people said 'Amen'" (1 Chronicles 16:36).

Help me, Lord, to know that because you are my Father, all men and women are my brothers and sisters.

CHAPTER 69

Joy in the Sanctuary

PSALM 100

> *Worship the* LORD *with gladness.*
> (100:2, NRSV)

"AMONG THE PSALMS OF triumph and thanksgiving, this stands preeminent, as rising to the highest point of joy and grandeur," states the eminent Bible scholar Franz Delitzsch.

Seven verbs in this psalm are commands, summoning us to joyful worship of our God. God does not invite us to come to him in joyful worship; he commands us to do so.

"Shout for joy to the LORD" (v. 1). C. S. Lewis observed that in the vibrant music of the psalms "I find an experience fully God-centered, asking of God no gift more urgently than his presence, the gift of himself, joyous to the highest degree, and unmistakably real. What I see in the faces of these old poets tells me more about the God whom they and we adore."

Worship is one of the most sacred exercises of life. It ushers us into the presence of the God who created the heavens and the earth. In worship, the creature comes to his Creator, the finite comes to the Infinite, a being of folly and sin comes to the One who is all wisdom and holiness. Yet, even in the light of these eternal realities, the psalmist does not call us to austerity. He tells us that there is a place for mirth in the sanctuary. His disposition was akin to Browning's:

> *I find earth not gray but rosy,*
> *   Heaven not grim but fair of hue,*
> *Do I stoop? I pluck a posy.*
> *   Do I stand and stare? All's blue.*

Such a perspective serves as a corrective to austerity and severity. God himself, in his Word, invites us to "shout for joy." May our places of worship, of preaching, praying, and witnessing, all echo the joyful tone of this psalm.

"Serve the LORD with gladness" (v. 2). One of the great privileges of our Christian life is that we can serve God. He has work for us to do. But, just as no earthly person in authority wants service rendered just mechanically or grudgingly, so the Lord of the universe wants our service rendered with gladness.

An unknown writer has challenged us: "I shall pass through this world but once. Any good thing, therefore, that I can do, or any kindness that I can show any human being, let me do it now. Let me not defer nor neglect it – for I shall not pass this way again."

The psalmist invites us to come before the Lord's presence with singing (v. 2). Singing has always been a hallmark of Christian worship. It is difficult to believe that there have been some Christians who at one time forbade singing in public worship, or the use of a piano. The psalmist finds a kindred soul in Isaac Watts, who wrote: "Let those refuse to sing,/Who never knew our God."

"Know that the LORD is God" (v. 3). God is not interested in a joyful noise that is devoid of any knowledge of himself. Our joyful worship must be tempered with reverence. Verse 3 reminds us of God's absolute sovereignty when it declares that "we are . . . the sheep of his pasture" (v. 3).

"Know thyself" is Socrates' wise aphorism. But to know God is a higher wisdom. May we grow in our knowledge of God, and in that knowledge may we love and adore and joyfully worship him.

God, my Creator and Savior, joyfully I come to you in worship and praise.

CHAPTER 70

Thank God

PSALM 100, CONTINUED

> *Give thanks to him.*
> (100:4)

THE WORD "THANK" COMES from an Anglo-Saxon word meaning "a thought." So, essentially, thankfulness is thought-fulness. When the psalmist thought about God, about who God is and what he does for us, there poured forth this irrepressible expression of thanksgiving. This is the only psalm bearing the inscription "for giving thanks."

Gratitude has been defined as "the memory of the heart." When we truly know God, we will remember his mercies and blessings toward us, and with the psalmist we will aspire to

> *Enter his gates with thanksgiving,*
>   *and his courts with praise;*
>   *give thanks to him and praise his name.*

(v. 4)

The essence of worship is thankfulness and wonder. Philosopher Gerald Heard described it as "that mixture of profound awe and overwhelming, self-forgetful delight which is the true catharsis and deliverance of the soul." Psalms of praise help to rekindle within us gratitude and reverence for God and a cherishing of the wonder of God himself and his relationship with humankind.

> *For the LORD is good and his love endures forever;*
>   *his faithfulness continues through all generations.*

(v. 5)

No wonder this psalm has the inscription "for giving thanks." Christian poets have beautifully adapted this psalm in hymns, including this paraphrase by William Kethe, set to the tune "Old Hundredth":

> *All people that on earth do dwell,*
>   *Sing to the Lord with cheerful voice;*
> *Him serve with fear, his praise forth tell,*
>   *Come ye before him and rejoice.*

> *The Lord, ye know, is God indeed;*
>   *Without our aid He did us make;*
> *We are his flock, he doth us feed,*
>   *And for his sheep he doth us take.*

O enter then his gates with praise,
  Approach with joy his courts unto;
Praise, laud and bless his name always,
  For it is seemly so to do.

For why? The Lord our God is good,
  His mercy is forever sure;
His truth at all times firmly stood,
  And shall from age to age endure.

Gracious God, help me to think on your glory and goodness and to have a heart overflowing with thankfulness.

CHAPTER 71

Home Religion

PSALM 101

> *I will walk in my house with blameless heart.*
> (101:2b)

HOME IS THE ULTIMATE testing ground of our religion. "It is easier," writes Adam Clarke, "for most men to walk with a perfect heart in the church, or even in the world, than within their own families." Dwight L. Moody said that if he wanted to know about a man's religion, he would not ask his minister, but his wife. A man's character is put to the test in the privacy of his own home, in the midst of those with whom he lives most intimately and for whom he is most responsible.

King David, who gave us Psalm 101, was a public figure. He was responsible for his royal court and the government of his nation and people. But public functions and the heavy demands of a king did not exempt him from his obligations to his family. David knew that a good father and head of a family would be a better king to his people. The same principles of guiding and nurturing a family apply to ruling a nation. Thus, in this psalm of a king's solemn purpose, he vows to "walk in my house with blameless heart."

In the seventeenth century, this was known as "The Householder's Psalm," and it would be read at the setting up of a new family or upon entering a new home. May we not lose the sense of sacredness in establishing a God-centered home. May we, with the psalmist, vow: "I will walk in my house with blameless heart." May none of those near and dear to us experience any lack of character, faithfulness, love, kindness, or goodness in our home relationships and responsibilities.

Our oldest daughter once wrote down the commitment of herself and her husband to their family and a Christ-centered home. A grateful set of parents and grandparents have been richly blessed by the results of that commitment:

The teaching of God's Word, the love for acquiring knowledge, and the example of living for Christ – these enriched my home as a young child and teenager. The Lord has given me so much and He now requires me to give much in return. I want my home to be a place that stimulates creativity, that offers opportunity for the study of music, or books, or hobbies, where ideas can be shared and questions safely discussed. I want Christ's presence to permeate our home. God is obviously a lover of beauty, color, simplicity, creativity. Our God is a God of serenity and refreshment. I want my home and my family to radiate this kind of God whom we serve.

During the administration of President Jimmy Carter, White House staff received a handwritten memorandum from the President. The Chief Executive took time to write to his top aides, urging them to spend "an adequate amount of time" with their families. Written on White House stationery and signed, "J. Carter," the memorandum read: "I am concerned about the family lives of all of you. I want you to spend an adequate amount of time with your husbands, wives and children, and also to involve them as much as possible in our White House life. We are going to be here a long time, and all of you will be more valuable to me and the country with a stable home life."

May we echo in our hearts and homes these sound convictions of a king and a president. May we never be too busy to invest time in the nurture of family life.

How goes it with your family? Is Christ the unseen presence, his love and goodness and purity the standard of life within your household? He wants to occupy every corner of our hearts and homes and flood them with his radiance and joy. He will make our home a shelter from the storms that assail it from outside, and a threshold of the heavenly home he is preparing for us.

Heavenly Father, help me to live a blameless life in my home and before my family.

CHAPTER 72

Overflowing Praise

PSALM 103

> Praise the LORD, O my soul.
> (103:1)

THIS PSALM HAS WON an honored place in the devotional life of the church and the Christian. It is one of the noblest hymns in the Old Testament, expressing in unforgettable language the celebration of God's mercies. God's creation of our world and his work of mercy in our lives deserve from us our lyrical praise, of which this psalm is a noble example. With uninhibited expression the psalmist exclaims:

> Praise the LORD, O my soul;
>   all my inmost being, praise his holy name.
>
> (v. 1)

David here addresses his soul (vv. 1, 2, 22b) in the conventional Hebrew mode. His nature, all his inmost being, is constrained to praise the Lord. Our praise to God must not be superficial, half-hearted words or mere emotions without thought. Let all that is within us praise the Lord.

Let our intellects praise him by meditating on his majesty. Let our affections praise him with an outpouring of our love. Let our desires praise him by our longing for his return. Let our imaginations praise him by considering his glory. Let our mem-

ories praise him by recalling the great things he has done for us.
Let our words praise him by truthfulness and goodness. Let our
acts praise him by kindness and integrity. Let all our senses, all
our strength, all our faculties – "all my inmost being, praise his
holy name."

The call to praise frames the text of this psalm. At its beginning and ending, and altogether six times (vv. 1, 2, 20-22), the
note rings out, "Praise the LORD." This psalm overflows with
praise and gratitude to God.

Praise is not offered in words or songs alone. Rather our
whole life is to be an expression of praise. Horatius Bonar, over
a century ago, caught and conveyed this truth in his hymn,
which serves well as our prayer in response to this psalm:

> *Fill thou my life, O Lord my God,*
> *In every part with praise,*
> *That my whole being may proclaim*
> *Thy being and thy ways.*
>
> *Not for the lip of praise alone,*
> *Nor e'en the praising heart*
> *I ask, but for a life made up*
> *Of praise in every part.*
>
> *Praise in the common words I speak,*
> *Life's common looks and tones,*
> *In fellowship at hearth and board*
> *With my beloved ones.*
>
> *Not in the temple crowd alone*
> *Where holy voices chime,*

But in the silent paths of earth,
    The quiet rooms of time.

So shall no part of day or night
    From sacredness be free;
But all my life, in every step,
    Be fellowship with thee.

(1866)

God of majesty and miracle, make all my life a paean of praise to you.

CHAPTER 73

"Forget Not"

PSALM 103, CONTINUED

Forget not all his benefits.
(103:2b)

MEMORY – WHAT A WORLD in a word! It has been called the most amazing cupboard ever devised. Aristotle aptly described it as "the scribe of the soul." It gathers our personal archives of mementoes of the great things God has done for us.

With good reason the Scriptures often exhort us to remember, not to forget. Forgetfulness atrophies the muscles of praise and gratitude. Let us be most careful to "forget not all his bene-fits."

No one has ever fully cataloged all that God has done for us, and no one ever could. But the psalmist helps us begin well by recalling some of God's great bounty of blessings to us. What an inventory he compiles. Spurgeon, in his description of this text, writes, "He selects a few of the choicest pearls, threads them on the string of memory, and hangs them about the neck of gratitude."

"He forgives all my sins," says the psalmist in gratitude. What an inestimable gift is God's forgiveness. Truly "forgive" is one of the most beautiful words of the Bible. Though we have re-belled, he forgives. Though we have chosen our way over his, he forgives. Though we have spurned his love, he forgives. Though we have transgressed his moral law of the universe, he forgives.

Forgiveness on a human scale involves one of the most pro-found acts of our spiritual lives. Alexander Pope, in his famous words, equates human forgiveness with divinity: "To err is hu-man, to forgive divine." In the musical *Hosea,* John Gowans be-queathed to us beautiful stanzas penned for the libretto, and since sung by Salvation Army congregations:

> *If human hearts are often tender,*
> *And human minds can pity know,*
> *If human love is touched with splendor,*
> *And human hands compassion show,*
>
> *If sometimes men can live for others,*
> *And sometimes give where gifts are spurned,*
> *If sometimes treat their foes as brothers,*
> *And love where love is not returned,*

> *Then how much more shall God our Father*
> *In love forgive, in love forgive.*
> *Then how much more shall God our Father*
> *Our wants supply, and none deny.*

The psalmist continues to list "choice pearls" on his "string of memory." He exults, "He . . . heals all my diseases" (v. 3). God heals the deeper afflictions of life. He cures our pride, which is a derangement. He stays our anger, which is a fever. He takes away our lust, which can be a madness in the brain. He heals our sin, which can destroy our souls for eternity. There are also many who can testify to God's healing of physical diseases, who have known the healing touch of the Good Physician. Miracles of healing have occurred that no physician could explain.

We are all included in the immortal words that express what God has done for us: "He redeems my life from the pit and crowns me with love and compassion" (v. 4). God redeems us. He has purchased our salvation through his great sacrifice of his Son on the cross.

"He satisfies my desires with good things, so that my youth is renewed like the eagle's" (v. 5). The eagle is the monarch of the air. It soars to heights unattained by any other. It builds its nest where no human feet have ever trod. Its flight is majestic as it glides amid the storms and tempests of heaven. Its remarkable vision can detect minute objects at great distances. Its unflagging strength, even in old age, symbolized for the psalmist how God renews our vigor.

Loving God, may I always be mindful of your boundless bounty of blessings.

CHAPTER 74

"Never the Twain Shall Meet"

PSALM 103, CONTINUED

As far as the east is from the west,
so far has he removed our transgressions from us.
(103:12)

"HE DOES NOT TREAT us as our sins deserve" (v. 10), says the psalmist. The reason God can do this is that he has treated Another as our sins deserve. There was Another who "was pierced for our transgressions . . . crushed for our iniquities; the punishment that brought us peace was upon him, and by his wounds we are healed" (Isaiah 53:5).

In the room that was Lincoln's office, and in recent years has become known as the Lincoln Bedroom, is an old Lincoln bed and a fireplace with a small bronze plaque on the mantel. The plaque reads: "In this room Abraham Lincoln signed the Emancipation Proclamation of January 1, 1863, whereby four million slaves were given their freedom and slavery was forever prohibited in the United States." With one stroke of the pen Lincoln freed those in slavery and forever banned it in the country. Christ, on Calvary, became the great Emancipator of our souls. In that one mighty act of sacrifice, he forever freed his followers from sin's bondage, giving us glorious liberty in the Spirit.

"For as high as the heavens are above the earth, so great is his love for those who fear him" (v. 11). The heights of God's love have never been scaled. Its depths have never been sounded.

His mercy toward us is without limit. Annie Johnson Flint has put this truth into verse for us to sing:

> His love has no limit, his grace has no measure,
>   His power no boundary known unto men;
> For out of his infinite riches in Jesus
>   He giveth, and giveth, and giveth again.

After describing the vertical dimension of God's love, "as high as the heavens are above the earth," the psalmist describes its horizontal dimension in one of Scripture's most unforgettable metaphors of God's forgiveness of sin: "As far as the east is from the west, so far hath he removed our transgressions from us" (v. 12). The popular lines from Rudyard Kipling's ballad remind us that "East is East, and West is West, and never the twain shall meet." The psalmist assures us that once we accept God's forgiveness, our sins and we will never meet again! God puts so much distance between us and our sins that we are utterly and forever separated from them. God's immense mercy that has taken away our sins is beyond all measurable dimensions.

The story is told that when Moravian missionaries first went to the Eskimos, they could not find a word in their language for forgiveness, so they had to compound one. They made up the word *issumagijoujungnainermik*. This formidable assembly of letters had a beautiful connotation for those who understood it. It means: "not-being-able-to-think-about-it-anymore." The forgiveness of God includes complete and eternal forgetfulness. Once we confess and repent of sin, God never brings it back against us. It is cast into his eternal sea of forgetfulness.

What a beautiful and blessed assurance this psalm brings to each of us. We too, with the psalmist, are filled with irrepressible praise.

Thank you, God, for your giving and forgiving, infinitely beyond my understanding.

CHAPTER 75

Remembered by God

PSALM 103, CONTINUED

> *For he knows how we are formed,*
> *he remembers that we are dust.*
> (103:14)

LIFE IS FRAGILE AND finite. The psalmist likens us to the flower that flourishes and then quickly fades away. Each of us lives only a couple of generations from oblivion, from being forgotten and unknown. But the psalmist declares that we are not forgotten by God: "He remembers." That alone becomes our claim to immortality.

> *For he knows how we are formed,*
> *he remembers that we are dust.*
> *As for man, his days are like grass,*

> *he flourishes like a flower of the field;*
> *the wind blows over it and it is gone,*
>   *and its place remembers it no more.*

(vv. 14-16)

Solzhenitsyn, in his autobiographical work *The Oak and the Calf,* calls himself "a transient meteorite." We are transient in our journeys as meteorites that flicker on the horizon and quickly disappear. But such a metaphor is only partially true.

The encouraging fact the psalmist declares is that God knows us. He remembers us. We shall become like his stars that shine forever. The infinite span of God's love overarches each person's brief moment of time. These are his assuring words:

> *But from everlasting to everlasting*
>   *the LORD's love is with those who fear him,*
>   *and his righteousness with their children's children –*
> *with those who keep his covenant*
>   *and remember to obey his precepts.*

(vv. 17-18)

The legacy of faith and remembrance by God is passed on to succeeding generations.

The closing verses refer to angels, one of the intriguing mysteries in the Bible. This psalm tells us: (1) they are the Lord's; (2) they excel in strength; (3) they do God's bidding; (4) they are holy, obeying his word (vv. 20-21). We have cause to believe that there are demons on the earth, but let us not forget this blessed assurance that God has celestial beings who do his bidding on earth among us.

All creation is called on to "Praise the LORD" (v. 22), for "his kingdom rules over all" (v. 19). May this psalm echo our radiant experience of lives overflowing with praise for his goodness and grace.

Henry Francis Lyte has paraphrased this noble psalm of praise for modern worshipers to sing:

Praise, my soul, the King of Heaven,
 To his feet thy tribute bring;
Ransomed, healed, restored, forgiven,
 Who like thee his praise should sing?
Praise him! Praise the everlasting King.

Praise him for his grace and favor
 To our fathers in distress;
Praise him still the same as ever,
 Slow to chide and swift to bless;
Praise him! Glorious in his faithfulness.

Father-like He tends and spares us;
 Well our feeble frame He knows,
In his hands He gently bears us,
 Rescues us from all our foes.
Praise him! Widely as his mercy flows.

(1834)

Eternal God, I am awed and humbled that my frailty is linked with your eternity.

CHAPTER 76

A Hymn to the Creator

PSALM 104

> *Praise the LORD, O my soul.*
> *O LORD my God, you are very great;*
> *you are clothed with splendor and majesty.*
> (104:1)

ONE BIBLE COMMENTATOR OBSERVES that the psalmist lived in "a universe aglow with God." The author of Psalm 104 has been called "the Wordsworth of the ancients, penetrated with a love for nature." In this lyrical hymn of creation, the psalmist presents a philosophy of the cosmos with the recognition of God's sovereignty and his providence in the world.

The "bookends" of this psalm resonate with praise, as it begins and ends with "Praise the LORD, O my soul."

The greatest occupation of the human mind is contemplation of the glory and majesty of God. There is no more lofty theme for us to contemplate. After considering the sheer greatness of God the psalmist says: "May my meditation be pleasing to him, as I rejoice in the LORD" (v. 34). May we with the psalmist have meditations upon our Creator that will be pleasing to him.

The psalmist begins with an acknowledgment of the greatness of God: "How great you are! Clothed in majesty and glory, wrapped in a robe of light!" (vv. 1-2, JB). C. H. Spurgeon writes of this verse: "Wrapping light about him as a monarch puts on his robe is a conception that is sublime. But it makes us feel how altogether inconceivable the personal glory of the Lord must be; if light itself is but his garment and veil, what must be the blazing splendor of his own essential being!"

The psalmist acknowledged God as the creator and governor of his world, deserving of the loftiest worship and praise. He praises the God of creation in vivid poetry. His imagery is freed from literalness, with storm clouds described as God's chariot, the wind his winged horse, and angels his ministering spirits:

> *He makes the clouds his chariot*
> *and rides on the wings of the wind.*
> *He makes winds his messengers,*
> *flames of fire his servants.*   (vv. 3-4)

Robert Grant, writing in the early 1890s, used this psalm as the basis for a hymn that has found its way into the hymnals of Christian churches around the world:

> *O worship the King, all glorious above;*
> *O gratefully sing his power and his love;*
> *Our shield and defender, the Ancient of Days,*
> *Pavilioned in splendor and girded with praise.*

> *O tell of his might, O sing of his grace,*
> *Whose robe is the light, whose canopy space;*
> *His chariots of wrath the deep thunderclouds form,*
> *And dark is his path on the wings of the storm.*

> *The earth with its store of wonders untold,*
> *Almighty, Thy power hath founded of old,*

Hath 'stablished it fast by changeless decree,
    And round it hath cast, like a mantle, the sea.

Thy bountiful care what tongue can recite?
    It breathes in the air, it shines in the light,
It streams from the hills, it descends to the plain,
    And sweetly distills in the dew and the rain.

(1833)

God, "pavilioned in splendor," your awesome majesty surpasses my finite mind and stammering words.

CHAPTER 77

From Wonder to Worship

PSALM 104, CONTINUED

May my meditation be pleasing to him.
(104:34)

THIS PSALM, A COSMIC Rosetta Stone, unlocks for us the mystery and majesty of the meaning of the universe. God is sovereign. He is the creator, and he has made the world purposeful. We are his creatures, totally dependent upon him, but assured of his providence for us.

Psalm 104 is a poet's version of the creation account of Genesis, following the order of creation. In awe and adoration, it praises the Lord of seven wonders: sky (vv. 2-4), earth (vv. 5-9), vegetation (vv. 14-18), moon and sun (vv. 19-23), sea (vv. 24-26), life (vv. 27-30), and the glory of God himself (vv. 31-35).

C. S. Lewis, writing on this psalm, sets out this concept: "Another result of believing in Creation is to see Nature not as a mere datum but as an achievement. God has given to his works his own character. God has laid the foundations of the earth with perfect thoroughness. In this great Psalm devoted to nature, we have not only the useful cattle, the cheering vine, and the nourishing corn, we have springs where beasts quench their thirst (v. 11), fir trees for storks (v. 17). In the Psalmist's gusto for nature, they are our fellow-dependents."

The simple lines of Cecil Frances Alexander express in familiar words the message of this psalm:

All things bright and beautiful,
  All creatures great and small,
All things wise and wonderful,
  The Lord God made them all.

He gave us eyes to see them,
  And lips that we might tell
How great is God Almighty,
  Who has made all things well.

(1848)

As the psalmist contemplates the wonders of God's creation, he is led to worship, and he exclaims, "May my meditation be pleasing to him" (v. 34). There is no higher or nobler exercise of the soul than to worship God. As we praise and worship, God steps out of his mystery into our history, and we move from our history into his mystery. Our worship of God lifts us out of our preoccupation with the temporal and gives us an eternal perspective.

Too often we substitute activity and program for worship, the dull and predictable for the tip-toe expectancy and awe-inspiring sense of the presence of God. William Temple has given to us a weighty definition of worship: "To worship is to quicken the conscience by the holiness of God, to feed the mind with the truth of God, to purge the imagination by the beauty of God, to open the heart to the love of God, to devote the will to the purpose of God."

We too, when considering the magnificence of God's creation, will be led from awe to adoration, from reflection to reverence, from wonder to worship.

Creator and Sovereign of the world, I come before you with inexpressible wonder and praise.

CHAPTER 78

Song of the Redeemed

PSALM 107

> Let the redeemed of the LORD say so.
> (107:2, NKJV)

THIS ELEGANT PSALM TESTIFIES to the way in which the ancient Word of God comes alive for each new generation and speaks with relevance to each time and need. God's Word is not limited to one time and place in history.

"Give thanks to the LORD, for he is good; his love endures forever" (v. 1) – this is the conventional call to praise by the psalmist. The redeemed of the Lord have cause to overflow with praise. The psalmist cites four different experiences of God's deliverance as cause for thanksgiving, each of which concludes with the same expression of praise: "Let them give thanks to the LORD for his unfailing love and his wonderful deeds for men" (vv. 8, 15, 21, 31).

This psalm sketches the spiritual biography of the redeemed children of God. "Some wandered in the desert wastelands" is the first example. They lost their way, wandered far from supplies of food and drink, and became exhausted. But they "cried out to the LORD in their trouble, and he delivered them from their distress" (vv. 4-9). Do we not identify with wandering in the wasteland and wilderness of sin, lost and desperate? But, in answer to our prayer, the Lord delivered us.

The second example depicts those in chains who languish in the darkness and gloom of prison. They too prayed and were delivered (vv. 10-16). Who of us has not known the chains and fetters that bound us until he set us free?

The third group suffered severe sickness and came to "loathe all food and drew near the gates of death." They too prayed and were delivered (vv. 17-22). And what of our many ills from which he has delivered us?

The climax comes in the final example, described in graphic imagery, of those who "go down to the sea in ships" (v. 23, KJV). As mariners, they encountered the peril of the sea. Their frail ships tossed and pitched with fury from the crests to the troughs of raging waves and "in their peril their courage melted away." The psalmist gives an all-too-familiar picture (for some of us) of seasickness: "They reeled and staggered like drunken men." He then adds what has become a proverbial expression for coming to the end of our resources: "they were at their wits' end." But these also prayed and were delivered, again demonstrating God's deliverance in answer to prayer and giving cause for our praise and thanks to God (vv. 23-32).

Were we not tossed about on the raging sea of life until we heard the Master of the storm speak to us his word: "Peace, be still!" (Mark 4:39)? Then, as the author of this psalm tells us, "He maketh the storm a calm" (v. 29, KJV). We, with the fishermen of Brittany of old, would pray, "Lord, keep us, for the sea is great, and our boat is so small."

Let us all – fellow travelers in the desert, prisoners, the infirm, and those tempest-tossed – as redeemed men and women give thanks and praise to our mighty and compassionate Deliverer.

Strong Deliverer, with the psalmist I give you thanks for your unfailing love and wonderful works in my life.

CHAPTER 79

The Cursing Psalms

PSALM 109

> *O God, whom I praise,*
> *do not remain silent.*
> (109:1)

IN SOME OF THE psalms, the spirit of vengeance and hatred strikes us in the face like heat from an open furnace. The worst is Psalm 109. This vindictive psalm seems to contradict the whole gospel and teachings of the New Testament.

The psalmist's maledictions upon his enemies include these and many more: "May his days be few" (v. 8); "May his children be fatherless and his wife a widow" (v. 9); "May his children be wandering beggars" (v. 10); "May his descendants be cut off" (v. 13). There are no less than thirty anathemas in this psalm. Indeed, it is the strangest psalm of all, and it seems out of place in this "devotional treasury of the ages."

Any serious study of the Psalms sooner or later has to encounter and reckon with these cursing psalms, which include Psalms 35, 52, 58, 59, 69, 83, 109, 137, and 140. Many readers recoil from reading these psalms. It seems so inconsistent with our concept of the Bible to read, "Happy is he . . . who seizes your infants and dashes them against the rocks" (137:8-9). This seems more vindictive and vitriolic than any pagan literature. Perhaps we all identify with the one word a devout writer wrote opposite this psalm: "mysterious." When we come to these cursing psalms we must acknowledge our perplexity, our inability to understand them fully.

It is even more perplexing to realize that this psalm was designed to be sung in the temple service, as indicated by its ascription, "For the director of music." Furthermore, it is not the ravings of a misanthrope, but "a psalm of David." David was noted for his mercy toward his enemies.

One interpretation is that this psalm, as quoted by Peter, refers to Judas Iscariot: "For it is written in the book of Psalms, 'May his place be deserted; let there be no one to dwell in it,' and 'May another take his place of leadership.'" Peter identifies these words, spoken by the Holy Spirit "long ago through the mouth of David," as prophetic of the fate of Judas, the betrayer of the Son of God (Acts 1:16-20).

We must also remember the historical context of these psalms. The psalmists lived in a world of savage punishments, of massacre and violence, of human sacrifice. But is it really so far removed from our world of the Holocaust, the war in Vietnam, terrorism, the slaughter of refugees, and "ethnic cleansing"? As C. S. Lewis writes, "We are, after all, blood brothers to these ferocious, self-pitying, barbaric men."

Have we never harbored a spirit of vindictiveness toward those whom we thought had done us wrong? In real life, who would want a persecuting tyrant, a perpetrator of atrocities, to live long? Who could lament the extinction of a Herod, a Nero, a Hitler, a Stalin, a Saddam Hussein, or an Osama bin Laden? Dietrich Bonhoeffer had to make a hard decision of conscience when he joined the German officers' plot to assassinate Hitler.

Philip Yancey, in his article "How I Learned to Stop Hating and Start Loving the Psalms," shares his insight into this genre of psalms:

I see the cursing psalms as an important model for how to deal with evil and injustice. I should not try to suppress my reaction or horror and outrage at evil. Nor should I, Rambo-like, take justice in my own hands. Rather, I should take those feelings, undisguised, to God. As the books of Job, Jeremiah, and Habakkuk clearly show, God has a high threshold of tolerance for what is appropriate to say in a prayer. He can "handle" my unsuppressed rage. I may well find that my vindictive feelings need his correction – but only by taking those feelings to him will I have that chance for correction and healing.

The absence of righteous indignation can be an alarming symptom. It was Martin Luther King Jr. who prayed, "Give me the indignations of Jesus Christ." Easy condoning may be as injurious as enacting vengeance. As someone has put it, "Better to agree with God's curses than the devil's blessings."

Above all, this psalm should lead us to the New Testament and to the sublime example and teaching of Christ on love and forgiveness. That is God's final word to us.

Holy and just God, save me from a vindictive or vengeful spirit.

CHAPTER 80

To God Be the Glory

PSALM 115

> *Not to us, O LORD, not to us*
> *but to your name be the glory.*
> (115:1a)

PSALM 115 MAY HAVE been written to celebrate some great deliverance of Israel from its enemies. The nation of Israel might have been tempted to flaunt their deliverance and give themselves all the credit. But the psalmist acknowledged that to God alone belonged the credit and honor. In a text that is applicable to all the blessings of God to each of us, he recognized the true source of the good that had come to the nation:

> *Not to us, O LORD, not to us [the repetition is for emphasis],*
> *but to your name be the glory,*
> *because of your love and faithfulness.*

The Israelites had apparently suffered some misfortune at the hands of their enemies, who scoffed, "Where is their God?" (v. 2b). Suffering in the world may still pose to believers the challenge of a God who seems indifferent. People today look at the horror of the Holocaust, the genocide in Bosnia, the famine in sub-Saharan Africa, the grinding poverty of the Third World, or the September 11 atrocity and ask the same question. If there is a loving God in the universe, where is he? The answer is given immediately by the psalmist: "Our God is in heaven," and he goes on to acknowledge the sovereignty of God (v. 3). Though evil and suffering, as a consequence of sin, may have temporary domain, because God is sovereign all events of history will have their ultimate fulfillment in him.

The opening statement by the psalmist reflects a proper avoidance of pride and a recognition that all glory is due solely to God. The temptation at such a time of victory is to boast, if not in our own merits, then at least in that of our leaders. See what we, or our forefathers or children, have done! Such vanity can be found even in churches that proclaim their virtuous records and achievements. But the true example is that of the psalmist. The deliverance that has come to us, the blessings we have received, the victories we have won – these are not our achievements but God's bounties. We may have been his instruments, but it was he who gave the vision and made the achievement possible. That is the note to maintain in all our national and ecclesiastical celebrations. Any honors ascribed to human beings are properly subordinate to the providence of God.

François de Fénelon, in his *Meditations and Devotions,* shares his own struggle with self-centeredness:

> I have always desired to impress others. I want their approval. I need to feel loved. I crave popularity. O God, when will I cease to be too eager for applause? All love and glory belong to you. I am ashamed of my desire for appreciation. Lord, punish my pride. I take the side of your glory as opposed to my vanity. As for the applause of others, you can give it or take it away as it pleases you. I want to be indifferent to such things. If there is anything in my reputation that will bring you glory, that is alright.

F. B. Meyer tells us one of the major discoveries in his spiritual life: "I used to think that God's gifts were on shelves one above the other, and that the taller we grew in Christian character the easier we could reach them. I now find that God's gifts are on shelves one beneath the other. It is not a question of growing taller, but of stooping down, to get his best gifts."

"I believe the first test of a truly great man," wrote the wise John Ruskin, "is his humility." Spiritual maturity is giving to God, not to ourselves, the glory due his name for any work of grace or achievement noted. Such humility basically is honesty, truthfulness. Spurgeon reminds us: "The higher a man is in grace, the lower he will be in his own esteem."

Almighty God, save me from ever seeking glory for myself, but help me with the psalmist to ascribe to you all glory and honor.

CHAPTER 81

A Threefold Deliverance

PSALM 116

> For you, O LORD, have delivered my soul from death,
> my eyes from tears,
> my feet from stumbling.
> (116:8)

PSALM 116 IS INTENSELY personal. The pronouns "I" and "my" occur in every verse except two. The opening declaration is "I love the LORD." People so often tell of their "loves" – for a sports hero or team, a food item, a movie, a television program. May we be as eager and spontaneous in expressing our love for God. Let us, like the psalmist, not be reticent in telling of our love for our most priceless treasure.

What a miracle the psalmist relates: "For Yahweh listens to my entreaty; He bends down to listen to me when I call" (vv. 1-2, JB). Imagine: the Creator of the universe, the Sovereign of the cosmos, hears our prayer. "He bends down" – what a mighty condescension! And that condescension is "to listen to me" – I can commune with Divinity! Brother Lawrence has defined prayer simply and profoundly: "Prayer is experiencing the presence of God." And George Buttrick gives his definition: "Prayer is friendship with God." What an inestimable privilege we have in prayer!

The psalmist's testimony of love and thanksgiving was born out of deep distress and anguish:

> *The cords of death entangled me,*
>   *the anguish of the grave came upon me;*
>   *I was overcome by trouble and sorrow.*
> *Then I called on the name of the* LORD:
>   *"O* LORD, *save me!"*

(vv. 3-4)

To suffer passes, but to have suffered never passes. The pain and distress will one day cease, but what we learn in those deep experiences can be our treasure forever. Misfortune never leaves us where it found us. The psalmist went through distress and anguish and a brush with death. In his desperation he called out, "O LORD, save me!" Now he is able to testify: "When I was in great need, he saved me" (v. 6). He summarizes what the Lord has done for him: "For you, O LORD, have delivered my soul from death, my eyes from tears, my feet from stumbling" (v. 8).

Do not these words express our gratitude for blessings in our own lives? We too have known this trilogy of blessings from God: his salvation – he has delivered our souls from death; his solace – he has comforted us in our tears; and his strength – he keeps our feet from falling.

The world of the psalmist, around 1,000 B.C., has given way to the global village of our twenty-first century. Advances in communication, transportation, and technology have radically altered the way people live. Distances that would have taken David days to traverse can now be covered by jet plane in minutes. David would not have been able to communicate much beyond the distance and speed of a chariot. Today the Internet makes communications instantaneous from around the world. Indeed, technology has dramatically changed our world.

But one thing remains the same: the speed with which we can reach God in prayer. Many of us take advantage of the marvelous communication available over the Internet. On any given day I may sit at my computer and read an e-mail message from Pakistan, another from Australia, yet another from Canada, and many from all over the USA. I have no understanding of how this marvel works, but I have faith that when I send an e-mail message to a distant point, it arrives there immediately, and without error, just as such mail comes to me.

If communication on a human level can be so instantaneous and marvelous, how much more so on the divine level. We, with the psalmist, can say of our petition to God, "He heard my voice." We, with the writer of this psalm, can experience the reassuring truth that God is still only a prayer away.

Though heaven may at any moment be besieged with millions of calls, we never receive a message saying, "All the angels are helping other customers right now. Please stay on the line. Your call will be answered in the order it was received." Or, "This office is closed for the weekend, please call again Monday." When we pray, we never receive a busy signal, nor is God's line ever down. The God of the universe maintains a listening ear to the prayers and pleas of his children in their time of need. Praise him!

Divine Deliverer, thank you for bringing me from death to life, from tears to joy, and from defeat to victory.

CHAPTER 82

Testimony of Thanksgiving

PSALM 116, CONTINUED

> *How can I repay the* LORD
> *for all his goodness to me?*
> (116:12)

THE BOUNTIFUL BLESSINGS OF God recounted in the early section of this psalm involve a responsibility. The psalmist asks: "How can I repay the LORD for all his goodness to me?" That question needs to be asked by every child of God. It is not enough just to take the great blessings of God in our lives without accepting a responsibility in return. Privilege entails responsibility; how much more when the privilege is conferred upon finite human beings by the eternal God.

May we with the psalmist also say, "I will fulfill my vows to the LORD in the presence of all his people" (v. 14). We, too, have vows to keep. We have made sacred promises to God. Some of us have entered into covenants. Let us be faithful and, before others who observe our lives, keep those sacred vows. God has been faithful to us. He has never gone back on any one of his many promises to us in his Word. The psalmist's commitment to fulfilling his vows in the presence of others was so strong that it is repeated in verses 14 and 18.

Our vow-keeping must inevitably involve the world around us. "In our era, the road to holiness necessarily passes through the world of action," wrote Dag Hammarskjöld in *Markings*. The late Secretary General of the United Nations thus reminded us that the Christian life is not private but social, not passive but active. The brokenness of our world confronts us daily, and our faith must be inextricably wedded to the needs of the world around us. Holiness without social concern is like a soul without a body, but social concern without holiness is like a body without a soul. One is a ghost, the other a corpse. Only when they are wedded together do we have a healthy, life-giving gospel.

The psalmist also says, "I will sacrifice a thank offering to you" (v. 17). For the psalmist and other worshipers of his day, thanksgiving to God involved sacrifice. May our thanksgiving to God be invested with that which has value. May it be more than a glib expression. May it cost us something. True thanksgiving is "thanks living."

Charles Wesley has paraphrased this closing response of the psalmist for us to sing:

What shall I render to my God
  For all his mercy's store?
I'll take the gifts He hath bestowed
  And humbly ask for more.

The sacred cup of saving grace
  I will with thanks receive,
And all his promises embrace
  And to his glory live.

My vows I will to his great name
  Before his people pay,
And all I have, and all I am
  Upon his altar lay.

> *The God of all-redeeming grace,*
> *My God, I will proclaim,*
> *Offer the sacrifice of praise,*
> *And call upon his name.*

Loving God, may my gratitude be expressed in faithfulness to the sacred vows of my life.

CHAPTER 83

Precious Death

PSALM 116, CONTINUED

> *Precious in the sight of the LORD*
> *is the death of his saints.*
> (116:15)

THIS BEAUTIFUL PSALM CONTAINS one more jewel with a radiant truth to be shared. "Precious in the sight of the LORD," says the psalmist, "is the death of his saints." What a comfort this verse is to the believer.

When God created the world, he looked upon the work of his hands and pronounced it good. But none of that handiwork was called precious in his sight. The death of the saints, however, is precious in his sight. The people of God are of far greater worth to him than all the planets and stars of his creation. What a blessed assurance that we are so precious to God.

In particular, the death of his saints is precious to God. Why is the death of the believer singled out? That is the moment in which the believer is received in the eternal embrace of his heavenly Father. It is the moment in which the soul goes from the toil of the world to the rest God has prepared, from the labors of the earth to the rewards of eternity, from the sorrows of this world to the eternal joys of heaven, from the temporal fellowships of earth to eternal fellowship with God and the people of God.

Though death may seem to be a calamity, it becomes a celebration for the believer. Death is not a terror but a triumph for the child of God. For the saint, death is a coronation, the last step of life that leads into the presence of God forever.

When Catherine Marshall's husband Peter, the famous Scottish preacher, was felled by a heart attack, he whispered to his wife as he was carried from the house, "See you in the morning, darling." Those were his last words. Later they took on a transcendent meaning. Indeed, after our night in this world, the morning dawns.

The deathbed confidence of martyrs and saints presents an unassailable witness to the truth of our text. Theirs is an eloquent witness that God does not leave believers when they come to cross over this threshold. As Dwight L. Moody was about to enter his homeland, he said, "Earth recedes. Heaven opens before me. If this is death, it is sweet. This is my triumph. This is my coronation day! It is glorious!" Before him, John Wesley rhapsodized as he stepped into eternity, "The best of all, God is with us!"

In a London cemetery stands a headstone with an unusual epitaph. It was erected by the famous pastor, Joseph Parker, for his beloved wife. He could not bring himself to write the word "died." Instead, he had inscribed the word "Ascended." The believer at death does not leave the land of the living to go into the land of the dying. Rather, he or she leaves the land of the dying to go into the land of the living.

Although Fanny Crosby was blind, she possessed a rare spiritual perception that enabled her to bequeath some of the most inspiring songs that grace our hymn books. She composed one that was so personal that for years she never shared it with others. One day at a Bible conference in Northfield, Massachusetts, Dwight L. Moody asked her to give her testimony. She quietly rose and said, "There is one hymn I have written which has never been published. I call it my soul's poem. Sometimes when troubled, I repeat it and it brings comfort to my heart." Many were deeply moved as she recited:

> *Someday the silver cord will break,*
> *   And I no more as now shall sing;*
> *But O the joy when I shall wake*
> *   And I shall see Him face to face,*
> *And tell the story saved by grace!*

Fanny Crosby, without sight during her earthly pilgrimage, had as her most cherished hope that in heaven the Master's face would be the first one she would behold. For each of us who knows Christ, death will become the most precious moment of all, for then we shall see our Savior and Lord face to face. And our homecoming will be precious in his sight!

Christ, the Resurrection and the Life, replace any fear of death with an expectant faith that sees dawn beyond dusk, star beyond mist, and light beyond the darkness.

CHAPTER 84

Petite and Powerful

PSALM 117

> *Praise the Lord, all you nations;*
> *extol him, all you peoples.*
> (117:1)

PSALM 117, THE MIDDLE chapter of the Bible, is in the heart of God's Word. It is the shortest chapter of the Bible. But let not its brevity belie its beauty and blessing.

Breadth and depth are not determined by the number of words. Some of the world's enduring messages are very brief. The Lord's Prayer, Psalm 23, Lincoln's Gettysburg Address – all are literary treasures that will last forever. Yet each of them is less than three hundred words and requires less than three minutes to utter. There is power in brevity when it contains excellence.

The Scriptures would lead us to more brevity than is common. Jesus used the illustration of two men who went into the temple to pray. The Pharisee's prayer was long, wordy, and worthless. The publican's prayer was only seven words – short, but effective. God commanded Jonah to preach just an eight-word sermon to Nineveh; a national revival followed in its wake.

This psalm is short in size but exceedingly large in spirit. It breaks forth from the bounds of Jewish exclusiveness and is a rare Old Testament anticipation of the universality of the Christian faith. It knows no barrier of race or nationality but calls upon all humankind to praise the Lord.

"No man is an island," preached John Donne, "entire of itself; every man is a piece of the continent, a part of the main." We are often tempted to make islands of our lives, idyllic retreats from the world of people and issues and responsibility. But the psalmist, along with John Donne, reminds us that there is no retreat from others in the world around us. No matter how different we are from each other, we are all part of God's creation. We are connected to each other, a family of nations.

The psalm's two verses have three messages. First, all nations are to extol the Lord. Second, "Great is his love toward us." And third, "The faithfulness of the LORD endures forever." These two brief verses proclaim universal praise, unsurpassed love, and enduring faithfulness. With Francis Tucker, we sing:

> Let every tongue confess with one accord
> In Heaven and earth that Jesus Christ is Lord
> And God the Father be by all adored:
>   Alleluia! Alleluia!

One further notable thing about this psalm: it occupies an honored place with the messianic psalms, being quoted by Paul in Romans 15:11 as a prophecy of the universal character of the gospel ushered in by Christ. Luther writes of this psalm: "This is a prophecy concerning Christ – that all peoples, out of all kingdoms and islands, shall know Christ in his kingdom, that is, in his Church."

"Praise the LORD" is a fitting response to the good news of this petite but powerful psalm.

Worthy are you, our Lord and God, to receive praise and honor from all your creation.

CHAPTER 85

Christ's Farewell Hymn

PSALM 118

> *The LORD is with me; I will not be afraid.*
> (118:6)

WARNER SALLMAN, THE CHICAGO artist whose specialty was painting portraits of Christ and scenes from the life of Christ, captured a sublime moment in his unique portrayal of the Upper Room. He departed from the traditional method of depicting Christ and his disciples reclining around the Passover supper. In his painting, Christ and his eleven followers are standing. There is a look of confidence on their faces. Outside that Upper Room await the shadows of Gethsemane, the travesty of the trials, the horror of Calvary. But the painting presents a moment of faith, courage, affirmation.

The artist, a devout student of the Bible, chose to depict the moment of which the Gospel narrators write, "When they had sung a hymn, they went out to the Mount of Olives" (Matthew 26:30; Mark 14:26). Both Gospels close the Upper Room account with this statement. If only we knew the words of that hymn!

But we do know the words they sang at that moment. At the Passover meal, the "Hallel" Psalms were sung, Psalms 113–118. They were psalms of praise. Every Jewish boy had to memorize these psalms. Psalms 113 and 114 were sung near the beginning of the meal and Psalms 115–118 at a later point along with Psalm 136.

The music of these psalms was the prelude to Calvary. These were the very words that were on the lips and heart of our Lord as he prepared to go to the cross. This psalm was the farewell hymn of Christ with his intimate company of disciples. It has a special message for every Christian.

What were some of the words Christ sang with his disciples that evening?

First this psalm expressed thanksgiving: "Give thanks to the LORD, for he is good" (v. 1). Betrayal had just entered into the ranks of his most intimate company. The struggle and agony of Gethsemane, the violence and ignominy of the cross, were waiting just outside the door. Our Lord was going out to face Calvary and death. Yet he expressed thanks to God in the words of this psalm. What a sublime example of how we can thank God in every circumstance and trial of life.

Soon or late, every life must leave the fellowship of the Upper Room and enter the loneliness and struggle of Gethsemane. When we come to those experiences of trial, how reassuring it is that we can call upon God and he will answer. With our Lord, we too may say in time of trial: "In my anguish I cried to the LORD, and he answered" (v. 5). He might not take the trial away, but he will give us his grace, give us strength to endure it, and bring forth ultimate good and blessing even from our tragedies.

How inspiring it would have been to hear Jesus and his disciples sing these words that rang out from their lips and heart on that night of nights:

The LORD is with me; I will not be afraid.
   What can man do to me?

(v. 6)

These words of courage and confidence were the prelude to Calvary. We can face the worst when God is on our side. Dietrich Bonhoeffer, Corrie Ten Boom, The Salvation Army's Major Yin, and a host of other heroes and heroines of the faith of our own day have testified to the truth of these words. We are never alone when we are in God's will. Our faith overcomes fear. We may suffer, but we will ultimately triumph, as did our blessed Lord, as affirmed in the words of this psalm.

Dear Lord, may I look to your Word and find there courage for the conflicts and testings of life.

CHAPTER 86

The Most Important Day

Psalm 118, Continued

> *This is the day the LORD has made;*
> *let us rejoice and be glad in it.*
> (118:24)

OUR MEDITATION ON THIS psalm takes us to verse 8, the middle verse of the Bible. This verse, in the center of God's Word, tells us where to put our trust: "It is better to take refuge in the LORD than to trust in man."

Verse 22 speaks prophetically of Christ's triumph over Calvary: "The stone the builders rejected has become the capstone." Peter quotes this verse, affirming that this stone (Christ) which was rejected has become the "capstone" or the chief stone (1 Peter 2:6-8). The psalmist exults in this great triumph of our Lord: "The Lord has done this, and it is marvelous in our eyes" (v. 23).

In fulfillment of this prophecy, we encounter the familiar verse:

This is the day the Lord has made;
   let us rejoice and be glad in it.

(v. 24)

Each new day comes to us as a precious gift from God, with the opportunity to use it for good and for his glory. Time is life, and we are constrained to "fill the unforgiving minute with 60 seconds worth of distance run." When we run out of time we will have run out of life. We can choose either to waste or to use and invest wisely the priceless gift of each new 24 hours. We can spend and invest this account any way we desire, but we must also accept the consequences of our choices.

The psalmist reminds us that every new day God gives to us is a cause for rejoicing. Today is the most important day of our lives. Yesterday is forever gone. Tomorrow may never come. But today is ours to live, to laugh, to learn, to labor, to love. An unknown poet has eloquently expressed this theme in "Salutation to the Dawn":

Look to this day!
In its brief course
Lie all the verities and realities of your existence:

The bliss of growth,
The glory of action,
The splendor of achievement.
For yesterday is but a dream,
And tomorrow is only a vision.
But today well lived makes every yesterday a dream of happiness
and every tomorrow a vision of hope.
Look well, therefore, to this day!
Such is the salutation to the dawn.

Life is exceedingly brief, even at its longest. With the poet, Andrew Marvell, we "always hear Time's winged chariot hurrying near." Each day we awake is an extension of our life, for we have no contract or lease for the future. May we awake to each new day with the buoyant faith of the psalmist – accepting it as a precious gift from the Lord and rejoicing in it.

Lord, this new day is your gift to me. What I do with it will be my gift to you. Help me to do something beautiful with it for your sake.

CHAPTER 87

The Best Treasure

PSALM 119

> *Your word I have hidden in my heart*
> *that I might not sin against You.*
> (119:11, NKJV)

THE WONDERS OF GOD'S Word fill the 176 verses of Psalm 119 – the longest song in the Psalter and the longest chapter in the Bible. Its verses comprise the single most complete treatise and testimony in the Bible on the subject of God's Word.

A story is told of a preacher who many years ago called at a poor couple's home in the mountains. On entering, he saw hanging on the wall a framed $1,000 bill. Surprised, he asked, "Where did you get that?" They replied, "A sick man stopped at our cabin years ago. We nursed him back to health, and when he left, he gave us that pretty little picture. It seemed such a pretty souvenir, we had it framed." They were astonished when told how much it was worth and what it could do for them in their poverty.

How much more tragic it is when people fail to avail themselves of the riches of God's Word. So many live in spiritual want and poverty when God would meet their every need through the riches of his Word.

This great psalm opens, as does the entire Psalter, with a beatitude: "Blessed are they . . . who walk according to the law of the LORD" (v. 1). The word "blessed" is plural, speaking of the multiplicity of blessing and enrichment that comes from heeding the Word of God.

This psalm speaks to us about the diverse wealth of God's Word. The Interpreter's Bible describes Psalm 119 as "the greatest tour de force in the psalter." C. S. Lewis says of it, "From the literary or technical point of view, it is the most formal and elaborate of them all . . . it is a pattern, a thing done like embroidery, stitch by stitch, through long, quiet hours, for the love of the subject. It is the language of a man ravished by moral beauty."

The memorable eleventh verse can be simply summarized and outlined as follows (NKJV):

"Your word" – the best possession,
"I have hidden in my heart" – the best place,
"That I might not sin against You" – the best purpose.

Today we are blessed with a profusion of excellent Bible translations and paraphrases, which have been valued aids for deriving insight and inspiration from the Word of God. However, there seems to be one fallout from the use of multiple translations. In earlier times when everyone used one standard translation – the King James Version – there was great emphasis on Bible memorization. People would memorize many verses and whole chapters of Scripture. Memory is said to be the sheath in which the "sword of the Lord" is kept. My own Bible study and teaching ministry were greatly enhanced by verses, chapters, and books of the Bible I committed to memory in those early days. I heartily subscribe to the new and improved translations but regret the loss of emphasis on and practice of memorizing the classic portions of Scripture. With the inspired author of this psalm, let us keep the Word of God in our heart, internalized as an integral part of our life.

John Burton's words have been sung for over a century by Christians who acknowledge the Bible as God's treasure for the believer:

> Holy Bible, book divine,
> Precious treasure, thou art mine;
> Mine, to tell me whence I came;
> Mine, to teach me what I am.
>
> Mine, to call me when I rove;
> Mine, to show a Savior's love;
> Mine art thou to guide my feet;
> Mine, to judge, condemn, acquit.
>
> Mine, to comfort in distress,
> If the Holy Spirit bless;
> Mine, to show by living faith
> Man can triumph over death.

Thank you, God, for the priceless treasure of your Word. I will keep it in my heart so I may not sin against you.

CHAPTER 88

The School of Truth

PSALM 119, CONTINUED

> *Open my eyes that I may see*
> *wonderful things in your law.*
> (119:18)

THIS IS A TEACHING psalm, designed to instruct Hebrew children in the superiority of God's law. It is made up of twenty-two strophes or sections of eight lines each. Since they had no books, the youth memorized long portions of Scripture. To make this long psalm easier to memorize, it was arranged as an acrostic, from A to Z – *aleph* to *tau* in the Hebrew alphabet. Each of the first eight verses begins with the first letter of the Hebrew alphabet, *aleph*; each of the second eight verses begins with the second letter of the Hebrew alphabet, *beth*; and so on through the twenty-two letters of their alphabet. Perhaps the author also wanted to symbolize that nothing less than the full range of language would suffice to describe the sacred Word of God.

This divine acrostic contains vital revelation for all believers about God, ourselves, our world, salvation, and our eternal destiny. The psalmist acknowledges, as do we, "your statutes are my delight; they are my counselors" (v. 24).

The psalmist helps us appreciate the vast treasure of God's Word in this extraordinary tribute. He refers to God's Word in all but four verses (vv. 90, 121, 122, 132) and uses seven different synonyms for God's Word: law, ways, precepts, statutes, commands, promise, and decrees. These different terms point to the rich diversity of revelation and the varied ways in which we can relate to God's Word.

The psalmist realized that the Word of God is a vast treasury and that he needed the illumination of the Lord to discover its riches. He prayed, "Open my eyes that I may see wonderful things in your law" (v. 18).

This psalm is obviously the expression of one who had a devout love for God's law:

> *I find delight in your statutes; I do not forget your word.*
>
> (v. 16, JB)

> *Your decrees are my delight.*
>
> (v. 24, JB)

> *Meditating all day on your Law, I love your Law!*
>   *how I have come to love it!*   (v. 97, JB)

Do we have a devout, fervent love for the Word of God? Is it this precious to us? Is it for us a source of delight? Is our love for God's law manifested by our faithful observance of it?

"Why do you read the Bible every day?" a godly woman was asked. She replied, "I read the Bible every day because I'm a personal friend of the Author." We love God's Word because we love God and this is his message of love to us.

Bernard Barton reminds us in this hymn of what God's Word is to us and prays that we may know its wisdom:

> *Lamp of our feet, whereby we trace*
>   *Our path when wont to stray,*

Stream from the fount of heavenly grace,
    Brook by the traveler's way;

Bread of our souls, whereon we feed,
    True manna from on high,
Our guide and chart, wherein we read
    Of realms beyond the sky;

Lord, grant that we aright may learn
    The wisdom it imparts,
And to its heavenly teaching turn
    With simple, childlike hearts.

Lord, grant to me a receptive heart to partake and to live by the timeless truths of your Word.

CHAPTER 89
- -

A Light for My Path

PSALM 119, CONTINUED

Your word is a lamp to my feet
and a light for my path.
(119:105)

GOD HAS NO ERASER on the end of his pencil, nor an "undo" button on his computer. What he writes never needs to be changed.

The Constitution of the U.S. had to be amended almost before the ink was dry, with the Bill of Rights, the first ten amendments added. Isaiah proclaimed: "The word of our God stands forever" (40:8b).

This psalm reminds us that its enduring truth has the most practical application to our everyday lives. God's commands are our constant companion – "for they are ever with me" (v. 98). God's law is our most precious possession – "a joy beyond all wealth" (v. 14, JB). It is our unfailing guide – "your statutes are ... my counselors" (v. 24). It is our very source of life – "Give me life by your word" (v. 37, JB).

The psalm addresses the timeless and vital question of how young men and young women can keep themselves pure. The young man whose inner life is passion-swept, with one tidal wave after another of fierce temptation, must have an anchor for life's testings, lest his moorings be snapped and he be driven rudderless out to sea. How shall he keep himself pure? The question has never been more urgent than in our day of permissiveness, exploitation, and the so-called "new morality," which is nothing less than the old immorality. The psalmist puts forth the burning question for every young man or woman and gives the needed answer:

> How can a young man keep his way pure?
>   By living according to your word.

                                                                        (v. 9)

The phrase "according to your word" recurs throughout this psalm. The Word of God sets the standards in our age of "situation ethics" and moral decay. It provides the absolutes amid the sea of relativities in which many flounder and are lost.

Jesus prayed for his disciples, "Sanctify them by the truth. Your word is truth" (John 17:17). Such is the cleansing power of the Word of God.

The psalmist acknowledges his need for divine guidance:

I am but a pilgrim here on earth:
How I need a map –
and your commands are my chart and guide.

(v. 19, LB)

We also need to pray this prayer of the psalmist: "Turn my eyes away from worthless things; renew my life according to your word" (v. 37). Other ways beckon: *via mundi* – the way of the world; *via carnis* – the way of the flesh; *via Satana* – the way of the devil. But God's Word will lead us in the *via Domini* – the way of God. This alone is the way to joy, peace, purpose, and life eternal.

God's Word gives the insight and perspective we need for life: "The entrance of your words gives light" (v. 130). Another well-marked text in many Bibles refers to the guidance of the Word:

Your word is a lamp to my feet
    and a light for my path.

(v. 105)

Those words were penned before the days of electric lights, when people often had to make their way in inky darkness and over rough terrain. The lamp would not illumine the distance ahead, but would light the way for the immediate step to be taken. God's Word gives guidance for each moment, each hour, each day.

In Saco Bay, Maine, there is a rock jetty that affords a protected channel leading from the Saco River into the bay. Tides there vary, with a six-foot or more rise or drop. During high tide the jetty is submerged and a mariner must set his direction by the coastal chart, not by what he can or cannot see, or he will end up on the rocks. On life's sea, which has its own rises and falls, we must set our course by the chart of God's Word, which warns us of life's perils and guides us on our way.

A progression can be traced in this psalm. It begins with its references to youth, then speaks as a pilgrim on the earth. It is a parable of life's pilgrimage, pointing to the fact that as we pass through its testing places we will find God's Word to be our source of light and strength. May we avail ourselves of this vast treasure God has so graciously given to us.

Divine Instructor, may I follow faithfully the light of your Word on my path of life.

CHAPTER 90

The House of My Pilgrimage

PSALM 119, CONTINUED

> *Your statutes have been my songs*
> *in the house of my pilgrimage.*
> (119:54, NKJV)

THIS PSALMIST COMPOSED A songbook out of God's commandments: "Your statutes have been my songs in the house of my pilgrimage" (v. 54, NKJV). The NIV renders this verse: "Your decrees are the theme of my song wherever I lodge." God's Word becomes the theme and the source of harmony for our homes in our earthly pilgrimage.

God's Word is like music to our lives. It exhilarates us amid life's toils, refreshes us amid life's tensions, and sustains us amid life's trials. His Word restores our spent energy, touches our deepest emotions, motivates our wills, and makes us receptive to the ministry of the Holy Spirit. God's Word is the devotional music of the soul, touching the chords of our spirit with heaven's harmony.

We recall how David's songs upon the harp were the only therapy that soothed King Saul when the evil spirits would come upon him. This power of music over the soul was described by Henry Wadsworth Longfellow:

> *Such songs have power to quiet*
> *The restless pulse of care,*

And come like the benediction
   That follows after prayer.

And the night shall be filled with music,
   And the cares that infest the day
Shall fold their tents, like the Arabs,
   And as silently steal away.

The music of God's Word in the heart and home is not a sporadic or transient melody. The psalmist testified that his soul longed for God's Word "at all times" (v. 20). His Word will dispense inspiration in both prosperity and adversity, in peace or distress, in strength or weakness. God's Word always accompanies the believer – in the hand, in the head, and in the heart.

If we lack understanding of God's ways and will, it is not because any pages are missing in the book he has given us. Rather, it is because we have not read and applied the pages that are there. Our deepest thirst for knowledge and hunger for wisdom will not be satisfied in the universities of the world. Only this vast treasury will unlock the secrets of what life is all about and how to live it.

Billy Graham's early biographer tells of Graham's struggle with the authority of the Bible at the outset of his ministry. In the seclusion of his mountain retreat he spent days in prayer and with his Bible. The life-changing moment for him came when he dropped to his knees, with his Bible opened before him, and prayed, "Lord, I take this book as your inspired word by faith." That consecration and unequivocal acceptance of the Bible as the very Word of God gave to Billy Graham his authority as the world evangelist who has preached the Word of God to more people than anyone in history.

When we accept the Bible as God's Word to us, we too will find power and purpose in doing God's will and work.

Our world and life are dominated by change. Many lose their way and drown in the sea of relativities that surround us. Human teachings and philosophies are fickle and changeable.

But this psalm affirms that the Word of God "stands firm in the heavens" (v. 89). It is fixed, unchanging, not subject to the powerful winds of change that blow across the landscape of our world. When all other possessions and treasures of earth have faded into oblivion, God's Word will still endure. It is inviolable, indestructible, immutable, eternal.

Lord, help me ever to avail myself of this vast treasury you give to us.

CHAPTER 91

The Traveler's Hymn

PSALM 121

> *I lift up my eyes to the hills.*
> (121:1)

As ONE EXPOSITOR EXPRESSED it, we have just left the vast continent of Psalm 119 and come now to the islands and islets of what are called the Songs of Ascents, or Songs of Degrees. These fifteen psalms, 120–134, are a miniature psalter in themselves.

They formed a collection for the use of pilgrims journeying to annual religious festivals. Worshipers sang these hymns on their way to the temple on Mount Zion or en route to a holy observance in Jerusalem.

Psalm 121 is a traveler's hymn. Before the Hebrew families would start out on their pilgrimages, they would sing these words as an affirmation of their trust in God. It is also a soldier's song, its imagery borrowed from the military life of that day.

The opening of this psalm is very personal: "I lift up my eyes to the hills." This psalm speaks of the personal pilgrimage of each life. We are all pilgrims. We are only "passing through" this life. Our life on earth is only a brief moment of our eternal existence. Too often our preoccupation with the temporal makes us lose sight of eternity. The word "pilgrim" has, for the most part, dropped out of religious speech.

John Bunyan's *Pilgrim's Progress* is popular not only for its literary genius but also because Christian's perilous journey parallels our own pilgrimage. Our own soul makes the journey, through crisis after crisis, struggling through the Slough of Despond, walking through Vanity Fair, always with the need to press on.

As pilgrims, we too need to affirm and pray this traveler's hymn by one who made the journey long ago. The need and trust it expresses are ever contemporary.

The poet Byron called the mountains and hills the "palaces of nature." For twelve years our family owned some acreage with a cabin on top of a mountain in the Catskills of New York State. It became a place of retreat from the busyness and daily duties and deadlines back in the city. How often we derived refreshment and restoration from a personal pilgrimage to the mountain, amid its sylvan hills and vistas over the distant valleys. There our children and grandchildren wandered on trails of delight and discovery. Sometimes a morning rendezvous with a nearby trout stream added to the day's refreshment and even to the menu of the day. In the mountain's majestic splendor and quiet solitude, we breathed deep drafts of the invigorating air, and our bodies, minds, and souls were renewed. From the heights, we returned with a clearer perspective and sense of purpose. Mountains seem to offer their special elixir of life for the pilgrim who ventures to them. Thus it was for the composer of this psalm.

Hills had a sacred association for the psalmist. Mount Ararat recalled God's preservation and special promise. Mount Sinai was the place where God gave Moses the Ten Commandments. At Mount Carmel God answered with fire and proved the sham of pagan gods. The psalmist may have had these hills in mind where God gave a special demonstration of his power.

We too may be prone to look to our hills of religion, the hills of past blessing, the hills of our tradition. But, with the psalmist, we too must look beyond these hills to the God who created them, the God who is the source of the blessings and heritage we have received. We need a fresh dependence on him each day. Let us, with the psalmist, lift up our eyes and our hearts to God.

Help me to realize, Lord, that I'm a pilgrim just passing through this world. I look up to you for guidance and strength to make it safely through.

CHAPTER 92

The Unsleeping Sentry

PSALM 121, CONTINUED

> *My help comes from the* LORD.
> (121:2)

THE ORIGINAL TEXT OF the Hebrew Bible had no punctuation –
no commas, question marks, and so on. But there were "question words," words that always indicated a question. "Where"
is such a word. That is why many newer translations pose the
second part of verse 1 as a question: "Where does my help come
from?"

These words pose a timeless question of humankind. They
echo the deep need of our hearts. How desperately we need
help. How utterly limited are our personal resources. How
great are our needs. There are sacred tasks for which I am so inadequate. There are those who are dear to me for whom I carry a
heavy burden. There are those who look to me for encouragement in their faith. I must not fail them. There are personal
needs for which I require wisdom. Where does my help come
from?

With the psalmist, we too can affirm: "My help comes from
the LORD, the Maker of heaven and earth" (v. 2).

There is great reassurance in the often quoted prayer:
"Lord, help me to remember that nothing is going to happen to
me today that You and I together can't handle." The God who
created the cosmos is my Helper. I will take my frail and finite

life and put it in his mighty hands. And he will be my Helper and my Keeper.

In the four couplets of this psalm, the key terms are "the LORD" and "watch over," each occurring four times. This repetition emphasizes the Lord's watchful care for us. Each of us is embarked on the pilgrimage of life, which is fraught with perils and testings. We continually need the Lord's guardian care throughout life's journey.

The pilgrims of that day faced a long and dangerous journey to Jerusalem. They would have to encamp in the desert and desolate places. At night, a sentry would keep watch over the encampment. There was ever the danger of attack by robber bands who hoped to enrich themselves by raiding pilgrim camps. One of the greatest risks was that of the human sentry falling asleep.

We are assured that the divine Sentry of our soul is always on guard for us: "He who watches over you will not slumber" (v. 3). We can depend on his guardianship against the deadly enemies of our souls.

The psalmist makes reference to the dangers of the day and the night: "The sun will not harm you by day, nor the moon by night" (v. 6). In that day of travel on foot, pilgrims faced the very real danger of sunstroke under the blaze of the desert sun. Some also believed in "moonstroke," connecting certain ills with phases of the moon.

No scorching sun, no smiting moon, no ill-fated star can harm those who are kept by the Almighty. Because the Lord is our Keeper, we are secure against all inclement influences that would assault our souls.

William Cullen Bryant, in his elegant poem "To a Waterfowl," beautifully describes the heavenly Father's guardian care over the waterfowl's long and uncharted journey. He writes of

"a Power whose care teaches thy way along that pathless coast."
Then when the bird is "swallowed up in the abyss of Heaven,"
he draws his lesson for himself and for each of us:

> Yet on my heart
> Deeply has sunk the lesson Thou hast given,
> And shall not soon depart.
>   He, who from zone to zone,
> Guides through the boundless sky thy certain flight,
> In the long way that I must tread alone,
>   Will lead my steps aright.

*Divine Guardian, how assuring it is to know that you are watching over
me so I need not falter or fail on my pilgrimage.*

CHAPTER 93

In His Keeping

PSALM 121, CONTINUED

> The LORD shall preserve you from all evil;
> He shall preserve your soul.
>   (121:7, NKJV)

A HUMAN BEING IS the most helpless creature of all. We are cra-
dled, cared for, and coddled for a year before we can even walk.

Throughout our life we are weak and dependent. Who will keep us safe? "The LORD is your keeper," the psalmist assures us (v. 5, NKJV). What a condescension, and what a supreme provision, that the Almighty, the Creator of the cosmos, keeps each one of us.

The Lord's care is stressed repeatedly in this psalm. The word for "keep" occurs six times in the original text of this psalm, translated once as "keep" and five times as "watches over" or "watch over" in the NIV. How much we need this assurance in our daily living and tasks.

This psalm does not promise that we will be spared from difficulties, danger, or even death. History shows all too well that any such concept is unrealistic. But the true promise of this psalm is this: "The LORD shall preserve you from all evil; He shall preserve your soul" (v. 7, KJV).

While studying at Temple University in Philadelphia, I would on occasion slip into the basement chapel of the famed old Baptist Temple. It is called the Chapel of the Four Chaplains and memorializes with a graphic mural one of the great acts of heroism in World War II.

Clark Polling was a preacher, the son of one of America's most distinguished clergymen and the father of a lovely family. He was called to serve as a chaplain during World War II. During those dark days, he wrote to his family and parents: "I know I shall have your prayers, but please don't pray simply that God will keep me safe. War is dangerous business. Pray that God will make me adequate."

The troop ship *Dorchester*, on which he was serving, was torpedoed off the west coast of Iceland. As the ship was going down, Clark Polling and the three other chaplains on board handed their life jackets to four servicemen. They were last seen on the deck of the slanting ship, with arms linked and hearts in prayer, while somewhere in the icy Atlantic four men were cheating death because of their sacrifice. That act of heroism became a national symbol of faith-inspired sacrifice. In that moment, the prayers for Clark Polling were abundantly answered. God made him adequate.

God will not always protect us from danger, but he will make us adequate for every testing and trial. He may not preserve us from difficulty, but he will preserve us from evil, and he will even bring blessing out of the brokenness of our lives.

Now and again we cross a threshold and feel constrained to pause, realizing that we are passing from one phase of life to another. It may be when we go off to college, leaving home with its intimacies and security and facing new associations and challenges. Another threshold may be when we enter the work world, leaving the familiar world of home or school to face a world that is often callous, competitive, or even cruel. Other thresholds may include marriage, the birth of a child, the loss of a loved one, or taking new directions in our life. Through all of life's changes, the Lord will be our keeper.

The major changes that occur in our personal lives and professions represent a "going out," a transition.

The LORD shall preserve your going out
And your coming in from this time forth,
And even forevermore.

(v. 8, NKJV)

The beautiful promise of this psalm's conclusion is that, for God's people, the last part of life's journey is not a "going out" but a "coming in." The end of time is eternity. The last step of life's journey leads us into the eternal presence of God.

God, make me adequate.

CHAPTER 94

The Family Psalm

PSALM 127

> *Unless the LORD builds the house,*
> *its builders labor in vain.*
> (127:1)

THIS PSALM SAYS SOME vital and beautiful things about family life. I was not surprised to learn that this psalm was sung at a friend's wedding.

A good carpenter can build a house, but only the Lord can build a home. The psalmist states the timeless truth: "Unless the LORD builds the house, its builders labor in vain." He alone gives the needed foundation and infrastructure for harmonious and holy living.

Today family breakdown has reached epidemic proportions. More than a thousand times every day, somewhere in the U.S. a judge's gavel falls and with two words – "Divorce granted!" – somebody's love story comes to an end. Statistics tell us that nearly half of marriages today end in divorce. "Happily ever after" has been quantified by the census to about seven years. The family in America has become an endangered species.

But when Christ is the head of the home, there is love, peace, positive communication, affirmation, empathy, compassion, forgiveness, honesty, loyalty, prayer, and unselfish sharing. Christ makes the difference. Arthur Arnott has expressed it in song:

> Home is home, however lowly,
> Home is sweet when love is there.
> Home is home when hearts are holy,
> Earth has ne'er a spot so fair.
> Jesus makes our home a heaven,
> Sacred in the fireside warm;
> After battling through the long day,
> Home's a shelter from the storm.

Those who have been blessed with children know that they make a home and family complete. They bring a special and incomparable joy and blessing. The psalmist tells us: "Sons are a heritage from the LORD, children a reward from him" (v. 3). The word "heritage" implies a great value and a sacred trust. Our children are our most precious possessions. They are the richest treasures of our lives. No material goods or gain can compare with their worth. The Living Bible paraphrases this verse: "Children are a gift from God." During a visit to see our beautiful new granddaughter, my son told me that her name, Lauren, means "gift from God." Every child is a precious gift from God to the parents. They are his great reward to us, to enrich and bless our lives.

Children are also our most sacred responsibility. They are the first priorities of our lives. The Lord holds us accountable for their spiritual nurture by training and example. They are our first field of evangelism. Senate Chaplain Richard Halverson once was led to pray before the august assembly of the U.S. Senate: "Forgive those of us who give family such a low priority. Help the Senators not to be so busy trying to save the nation that they let their children go to hell."

Each child is a gift from God, but "for a limited time only." A parent has about eighteen years to raise a child, amid the external pressures of our world today. In that short space of time there are two lasting bequests we can give our children – roots and wings.

The psalmist uses a striking and felicitous figure of speech from his day:

> *Like arrows in the hands of a warrior*
> *   are sons born in one's youth.*
> *Blessed is the man*
> *   whose quiver is full of them.*

(vv. 4-5)

In the psalmist's day, true and trusted arrows were symbols of power and security. They were used for protection as well as for acquiring food. Poor indeed was the man of that day whose quiver was bereft of arrows. The psalmist employs this analogy to affirm that children are a blessing, enriching and enhancing life.

Thank you, Lord, for the precious and priceless blessing of family and home.

CHAPTER 95

National Security

PSALM 127, CONTINUED

> *Unless the LORD watches over the city,*
> *the watchmen stand guard in vain.*
> (127:1b)

THE LATE FRANCIS SCHAEFFER, who was deeply concerned about the future of our society, said that we seem determined to kill ourselves with abortion, euthanasia, the arms race, and moral decadence.

Mark Hatfield, former senator from Oregon and a devout evangelical, once offered this penetrating truth regarding the ills and crises of our society and world: "As a senator, I am dealing with political, economic, social, military and international problems. The attempt to find a political or economic answer to a spiritual problem will never work. Fundamentally these are spiritual problems."

The psalmist reminds us: "Unless the LORD watches over the city, the watchmen stand guard in vain" (v. 1b). The key word "vain" rings out three times in the first two verses, emphasizing the futility of earthly ways. Christ has the answer – Christ *is* the answer – to the needs and crises of our world today.

There is a little-known inscription in the dome of our Capitol in Washington, which reads: "One far-off divine event toward which the whole creation moves." A visitor saw this inscription and asked the guide what it meant. "I think," he said, "it refers to the Second Coming of Christ." Apparently, when the dome of our Capitol was erected, some official who believed this truth to be vital to our nation had the inscription etched in the dome of our seat of government. We need today, more than ever, to be reminded that our nation will be strong only if it is built on the foundation of faith in God.

During the Civil War, Abraham Lincoln issued a proclamation for a National Day of Fasting on the 30th of April, 1863. Calling the nation to a day of national humiliation, fasting, and prayer, he wrote:

> It is the duty of nations as well as of men to own their dependence upon the overruling power of God; to confess their sins and transgressions in humble sorrow, yet with assured hope that genuine repentance will lead to mercy and pardon; and to recognize the sublime truth announced in the Holy Scripture and proven by all history, that those nations only are blessed where God is the Lord. Intoxicated with unbroken success, we have become too self-sufficient to feel the necessity and too proud to pray to the God who made us.

This presidential proclamation is all the more needed and timely in this day when many would lead our nation away from its moral foundations and its fidelity to the Word of God.

Paul Harvey, the eminent newscaster, in one of his memorable radio addresses told what he thought he would do if he were the devil. The following are excerpts:

- I would promote an attitude of loving things and using people, instead of the other way around.

- I would dupe entire states into relying on gambling for their state revenue.
- I would convince people that character is not an issue when it comes to leadership.
- I would make it legal to take the life of unborn babies.
- I would take God out of the schools, so that even the mention of his name would be grounds for a law suit.
- I would come up with drugs that sedate the mind and target the young as users.
- I would attack the family, the backbone of any nation. I would make divorce acceptable and easy – even fashionable. If the family crumbles, so does the nation.
- I would persuade people that church is irrelevant and out of date, and the Bible is for the naive.

Like the psalmist, this newscaster, who has often been a prophetic voice to our nation, reminds us that we need the overruling guidance and government of God in our homes, our society, and our nation or, indeed, all is vain.

Creator and Governor of the universe, help us to have "In God we trust," not just as a slogan, but as a principle and practice.

CHAPTER 96

The Omniscient God

Psalm 139

> *You are familiar with all my ways.*
> (139:3b)

The Interpreter's Bible offers this assessment of this great psalm: "This is not only one of the chief glories of the psalter, but in its religious insight and devotional warmth, it is among the noblest passages of the Old Testament."

The psalmist is deeply impressed with three attributes of God: his omniscience – God knows everything (vv. 1-6); his omnipresence – God is everywhere (vv. 7-12); and his omnipotence – God is all-powerful (vv. 13-16). But he does not think of them so much as formal attributes as what he has found to be true in his personal experience. These awesome attributes of God are not expressed in abstract or metaphysical terms but in the context of personal life. The theology of this psalm is applied theology.

C. S. Lewis graced the world with his wonderful *Chronicles of Narnia,* a series of children's books widely enjoyed by children of all ages. In the first volume, *The Lion, the Witch and the Wardrobe,* in the enchanted land of Narnia, Lucy meets a majestic lion named Aslan, who represents Christ throughout the *Chronicles.* In *Prince Caspian,* one of the later books, when Lucy encounters him again, she says, "Aslan, you're bigger."

"That is because you are older, little one," answered he.

"Not because you are?" asks Lucy.

"I am not," says Aslan. "But every year you grow, you will find me bigger."

We share Lucy's experience. God doesn't change; rather, our knowledge of him expands. He is immutable. His character and his being are without diminution or augmentation.

Meister Eckhart (1260-1329), philosopher and theologian, would have us "sink deeply into the ineffable depths of the unfathomable ocean that is God." Perhaps we don't use words such as "ineffable" and "unfathomable" often enough in our contemplation of God. In this psalm we are led to consider three of the "ineffable" and "unfathomable" attributes of God.

The psalmist acknowledges God's complete knowledge of him: "O Lord, you . . . know everything about me" (v. 1, LB). He knows what we do: "You know when I sit" (my quiet hours, my moments when I am separated from the busy world) "and when I rise" (my busyness, my endeavors, my activity). He knows what we think: "You perceive my thoughts from afar" (v. 2). Even those nearest and dearest to me do not know my thoughts. My mind is a private castle with an uncrossable moat, unless I allow entry. But God knows my innermost thoughts. He knows what we say: "Before a word is on my tongue you know it completely" (v. 4). God has a window into every person's heart and thought.

God Almighty, by his very essence and nature, must be an omniscient God. Strike out that attribute and we extinguish his deity by a single stroke. The psalmist is overwhelmed by his contemplation of God's knowledge of him: "Such knowledge is too wonderful for me, too lofty for me to attain" (v. 6).

We do not pass through this world in unseen obscurity. God knows us better than we know ourselves. He knows us inside and out. Every detail of our life is known to him. He knows our every weakness, our every need, and he knows our potential through his grace.

I have often been amazed at how quickly we lose sight of humans on the earth when we take off in an airplane, until gradually we ascend to a height that renders everything on the ground lilliputian and indistinct. Imagine the inconceivable immensity of light-years that span the universe – and yet the psalmist says that God sees us and knows all about us.

Miracle of miracles, the God of the universe, who knows every star by name among their innumerable company in the fathomless depths of the cosmos – this same God knows me, everything I do, my very thoughts! We are honored if some great or famous person knows us. But what status is bestowed upon us to be known by God and to be loved by him!

Omniscient God, you who know me so utterly, may I come to know you better.

CHAPTER 97

The Omnipresent God

P SALM 139, C ONTINUED

> *Where can I go from your Spirit?*
> (139:7)

S OMEONE ONCE ASKED, "Where is God?" The discerning reply was, "Where is he not?" There is not a particle of this vast universe that is not filled with God. The psalmist knew that there was no place he could go and be away from the presence of God. He expresses it in the immortal words of Scripture.

> *Where can I go from your Spirit?*
>   *Where can I flee from your presence?*
> *If I go up to the heavens, you are there;*
>   *if I make my bed in the depths, you are there.*
> *If I rise on the wings of the dawn,*
>   *if I settle on the far side of the sea,*
> *even there your hand will guide me,*
>   *your right hand will hold me fast.*
>
> (vv. 7-10)

There is no escape from God. History books and biographies are filled with accounts of men and women who tried to escape from God but found that, wherever they tried to flee, God was there. Adam and Eve tried to hide from God in Eden. Moses fled to the backside of the Midian desert, only to find God pursuing him even in the brush of the wilderness. Jonah's flight ended with God finding him in the storm at sea and in the belly of the great fish. Augustine tried to flee God in worldly indulgence, but was compelled to confess that he could find his peace only in God. John Newton lived a profligate life, but even as he was sailing his slave ship God found him, and he testified to that experience in his renowned song, "Amazing Grace." Lew Wallace started to write a book to prove the falsity of Jesus Christ, but as he wrote a conviction started to haunt him, then a certainty gripped him. At 50 years of age he prayed for the first time; he became a follower of Christ and rewrote his manuscript, giving to the world *Ben Hur* to testify to the divinity of Christ.

Francis Thompson describes God's relentless pursuit of him in the unforgettable words of his poem "Hound of Heaven":

> *I fled Him, down the nights and down the days;*
> *I fled Him, down the arches of the years;*
> *I fled Him, down the labyrinthine ways*
> *Of my own mind; and in the mist of tears*
> *I hid from Him.*

In the end, Thompson meets and surrenders to the One who says, "I am He whom thou seekest!" God in his love seeks every life for himself.

If we were to paraphrase the psalmist's impressions of the omnipresent God using modern-day images, the result might be something like this: "If I take the wings of the Concorde or the Boeing 737 and fly to the uttermost parts of the earth, you are there. Or if I take the *Columbia* space shuttle and fly above the fingers of earth's gravity, or even make my way to the moon or other planets, even there your hand will hold me."

Blessed assurance, we can never drift beyond the love and care of our omnipresent God. Our heavenly Father is the God who is always near us. He pursues us in different ways – in the whispering of conscience, in the call of duty, in moments of tenderness and sorrow, in the crises of life, by a faithful example, by insights of his Word. He is the God of love who always seeks us for himself.

Omnipresent God, I am comforted to know that I am never out of your presence and care.

CHAPTER 98

The Omnipotent God

PSALM 139, CONTINUED

> *For you created my inmost being;*
> *you knit me together in my mother's womb.*
> (139:13)

AFTER DESCRIBING HIS PERSONAL experience of God's omniscience and omnipresence, the psalmist now speaks of his experience of the omnipotent God (vv. 13-18). "For you created my inmost being," declares David, "you knit me together in my mother's womb." The word translated "knit together" literally means "to interweave." It speaks of an intricate creative process. Paraphrasing the words of the psalmist: "When I was just an embryonic speck, you took charge of me and wove together my bodily frame."

Contemplating the marvel of the human body as created by God, the psalmist exclaims: "I praise you because I am fearfully and wonderfully made" (v. 14). This text has become a rallying cry for pro-life advocates in opposing the holocaust of abortion. God has created and knows the life that is in the womb, giving it sacredness and sanctity. The omniscient God who knows us and the omnipresent God who is all around us is also the omnipotent God who has created us.

The psalmist, in his pre-scientific age, exclaimed in wonder at the marvelous way God had made him. What would he say if he knew all that medical science has revealed about the marvel of the brain, the miracle of the eyes, the magnificence of the blood? Our livers make chemicals in exact mixtures and balances that are the envy of well-equipped chemistry labs – and do so day and night with no effort on our parts. Our hearts are amazing engines that beat 70 times a minute, 4,000 times an hour, 100,000 times a day. And what about our built-in immune system that attacks infection? All the discoveries of medical science underscore the psalmist's assertion a thousandfold.

We take for granted the marvels of God within our own bodies. We do not have to say to our pulse, "For heaven's sake, beat!" Or to our heart, "Don't forget to pump, 75 quarts an hour!" Or to each drop of blood, "Keep circulating through my 60,000 miles of blood vessels once every three minutes." Or to the eyelids, "Don't forget to blink."

Centuries ago Augustine reminded us that "Men go abroad to wonder at the height of mountains, at the huge waves of the sea, at the long courses of the river, at the vast compass of the ocean, at the circular motion of the stars; and they pass by themselves without wondering."

The omnipotent God, who flaunts his power in orbiting spheres, also displays his creative power in our individual lives. A loving, divine Craftsman fashioned the genes, chromosomes, RNA, and DNA into the marvel of life beyond our comprehension. Wonder of wonders, this omnipotent God comes to the door of our human hearts, knocks, and seeks admission. And where our strength ends, there God's omnipotence begins.

The psalmist tells us that God is not only the God of creation but also the God of re-creation. He is the God who will search our hearts and make them new, that we may have life everlasting. The psalmist would lead us to pray with him:

> Search me, O God, and know my heart;
>   test me and know my anxious thoughts.
> See if there is any offensive way in me,
>   and lead me in the way everlasting.

(vv. 23-24)

Self-examination is painfully difficult. Christian psychologist James Dolby says that "some people would rather die than be known. To be honest with ourselves is not natural." How courageous was the psalmist in asking God to search him.

We have been reminded by this majestic psalm that we have an omniscient God who gives us wisdom, an omnipresent God who is always with us, an omnipotent God who gives us power, and an all-loving God who leads us in the way everlasting. Praise him!

Omnipotent God, dispel my weakness with your strength, my feeble effort with your mighty power.

CHAPTER 99

The Hallelujah Psalm

PSALM 150

> *Praise the LORD.*
> (150:1)

TO USE A SALVATION ARMY term, Psalm 150 is the "hallelujah windup" of this great book that Martin Luther called "the little Bible." The flow of the broad river of the book of Psalms ends in a cataract of praise and unbounded exultation. The word "praise" is repeated thirteen times in six verses. W. S. Plumer, an authority on the Psalms, writes: "In this closing psalm, we see the almost inarticulate enthusiasm of the lyric poet."

What more appropriate ending to the magnificent Psalter could there be than this exultant call to praise. The original words are written in the plural, calling us all to praise. The elevenfold exhortation is framed by "Praise the LORD," or its equivalent, "hallelujah," a Hebrew word that has gone everywhere the gospel has gone and has become the universal word of praise and worship.

We are prone to chronicle our complaints, but too often we neglect to sound forth praises for what God has done for us. This psalm is a universal call to praise as it brings the entire book of Psalms to a hallelujah climax.

> *Praise the LORD.*
> *Praise God in his sanctuary;*
>   *praise him in his mighty heavens.*   (v. 1)

"His sanctuary" can refer to our offering of praise in corporate worship. What spiritual exhilaration fills, floods, and overflows the soul as we praise God together in his house! Praise gives wings to our souls, lifting us to new heights of communion and joy.

But, of course, the whole earth is his temple! There are so many occasions that call us to praise – the glory of a sunrise, the majesty of a star-studded sky, the flight of a sea gull, the kaleidoscopic beauty of a garden, the refrain of a melody, the touch of a loved one.

> *Praise him for his acts of power;*
>   *praise him for his surpassing greatness.*

(v. 2)

"His acts of power" stagger the imagination. Elsewhere the psalmist tells us, "The heavens declare the glory of God." The psalmist lived in pre-Copernican days when the earth was considered the center of the universe. The psalmist, in his day, was only able to see with the naked eye about 5,000 twinkling lights in the night sky. But through use of the modern telescope, astronomers compute that there are some 100 billion galaxies, each with, on an average, 100 billion stars. Astronomer Carl Sagan stated that the total number of stars in the universe is greater than all the grains of sand on all the beaches of planet earth. The fathomless thoroughfares of stellar space boggle the mind. We cannot but praise God for his "acts of power."

But, of course, we praise him most of all for his power in our lives, for "his surpassing greatness." We praise him for his infinite love bestowed upon us, mightily expressed in the unspeakable sacrifice of his own Son on our behalf. His love is continually manifest in his providence for us, both materially and spiritually. We praise him not only because he is a God of mighty power, but because he is also a God of infinite love. He is the Sovereign who became our Savior.

Francis of Assisi was called "God's Troubadour." His life was marked by a carefree, exuberant abandonment toward God. He tramped the villages and towns in the Middle Ages, joyfully announcing the kingdom of God, preaching it even to the birds along the way. His life was a paean of praise to his Creator, and for almost a millennium now his song, found in Christian hymnals around the world, has invited God's children everywhere to join with him in praise:

> *All creatures of our God and King,*
> *Lift up your voice and with us sing*
>   *Alleluia, alleluia!*
> *Thou burning sun with golden beam,*
> *Thou silver moon with softer gleam:*
>   *O praise him, O praise him,*
>   *Alleluia, alleluia, alleluia!*

God of might and majesty, with the psalmist of old I praise you for your surpassing greatness.

CHAPTER 100

God's Symphony of Praise

PSALM 150, CONTINUED

> *Let everything that has breath praise the LORD.*
> (150:6)

IT TAKES MANY kinds of musical instruments to make up a symphony. The harmony would not be complete if there were only drums or only trumpets. The psalmist, in verses 3-5, calls for the blending of the sweet music of the strings, the brilliant tones of the trumpets, the plaintive melody of the woodwinds, and the triumphant sound of the drums and cymbals. God invites us in our individual ways to praise him, thus contributing to his symphony of praise.

The psalmist invites us to praise the Lord "with the timbrel and dance" (v. 4, NKJV). Salvationists have long taken seriously the injunction to praise the Lord with the timbrel. In recent times we have begun to praise the Lord with dance in the form of creative choreography, often by young women, to the accompaniment of devotional music. Some of our granddaughters have blessed us with their ballet style dance of praise to the Lord.

"Let everything that has breath praise the LORD. Praise the LORD" (v. 6). Think of yourself as one of the instruments in God's great symphony. He doesn't expect everyone to praise him the same way or at the same volume. The important thing is for each of us to put ourselves at the disposal of the Great Conductor and to appreciate others who praise him in different ways.

St. Francis of Assisi echoes the grand theme of this climactic psalm:

Let all things their Creator bless,
And worship him in humbleness,
  O praise him, alleluia!
Praise, praise the Father, praise the Son,
And praise the Spirit, Three in One.
  O praise him, O praise him,
  Alleluia, alleluia, alleluia!

As C. S. Lewis writes in his *Reflections on the Psalms*, "All enjoyment spontaneously overflows into praise. The world rings with praise – lovers praising [one another], readers their favourite poet, walkers praising the countryside, players praising their favourite game. . . . The delight is incomplete until it is expressed." In heaven, our worship and our joy will be complete. Meanwhile, "we are merely, as Donne says, tuning our instruments."

One can imagine that the psalmist, in writing this closing lyric, was expressing feelings similar to those of composer Joseph Haydn, who said, "When I think of God, my heart is so full of joy that the notes leap and dance as they leave my pen."

As this psalm brings us to the end of the "finished symphony" of the Psalter, may we each "tune our instruments" for the grand symphony of heaven by praising God for all he is and all he has done. In the concluding words of the Authorized Version, "Praise you the Lord."

Eternal God, may the Holy Spirit be the conductor of my life so my whole being will be a symphony of praise to you.

Appendix

CATEGORIES OF PSALMS

The majority of psalms fall into one of the following categories.

Acrostic psalms
poems in which each new section, verse, or line begins with a successive letter of the Hebrew alphabet (examples: Psalms 9, 10, 25, 34, 37, 111, 112, 119, 145)

Cursing or imprecatory psalms
psalms that express indignation and vindictiveness toward enemies and call for God's swift and violent retribution (examples: Psalms 35, 49, 52, 58, 59, 69, 83, 109, 137, 140)

History psalms
accounts of specific events in Israel's history, including highlights of practically all of Israel's history (examples: Psalms 78, 105, 106, 136)

Messianic psalms
prophetic songs describing the coming Messiah as King (examples: Psalms 2, 24, 110), Servant and Savior (examples: Psalms 22, 40, 69), and Son of God (example: Psalm 118)

Penitential and lament psalms

psalms addressed to God in a time of personal distress or failure or a time of national calamity; they usually include a description of the problem, a confession of trust, and a vow of praise to God (examples: Psalms 18, 27, 44, 51, 62, 74, 79, and others)

Pilgrim psalms

songs sung by worshipers on their way to Jerusalem for annual feasts (examples: Psalms 120–134)

Praise psalms

psalms focusing on the word "praise" or "hallelujah"; joyful expressions of adoration for God (examples: Psalms 113, 117, 146–150)

Royal psalms

psalms that describe the King, both earthly and heavenly, reigning over his kingdom (examples: Psalms 2, 18, 20, 95, 96, and others)

Thanksgiving psalms

psalms that acknowledge God's unfailing love and express confidence in his promise for the future (examples: Psalms 18, 27, 62)

POETRY IN THE PSALMS

The psalms are largely written in poetry, not in the familiar rhyming of words, but in the Hebrew mode of rhymed ideas. Most verses in the Psalter are composed of two lines that "rhyme" their thought. There are five kinds of such rhyming, or parallelism, in the book of Psalms.

1. Synonymous parallelism
The second line repeats the thought of the first:

> The heavens declare the glory of God;
> the skies proclaim the work of his hands.   (19:1)

2. Antithetic parallelism
The thought expressed in the first line is contrasted with the thought of the second line:

> For the LORD watches over the way of the righteous,
> but the way of the wicked will perish.   (1:6)

3. Synthetic parallelism
The second line adds to and completes the thought of the first line:

> The LORD is my shepherd;
> I shall not want.   (23:1)

4. Emblematic parallelism
The first line uses a word picture to illustrate the thought given in the second line:

> As the deer pants for streams of water,
> so my soul pants for you, O God.   (42:1)

5. Climactic parallelism
The thought of the second line expands and reinforces the idea of the first line:

> Ascribe to the LORD, O mighty ones,
> Ascribe to the LORD glory and strength.   (29:1)

WORD PICTURES IN THE PSALMS

In addition to parallelism, the psalms include figures of speech – words or phrases used in a picturesque way for contrast, comparison, emphasis, or clarification. These word pictures serve to convey abstract concepts and difficult ideas through concrete images.

The following are some of the kinds of figurative language found in the book of Psalms.

Simile

a stated comparison between two things that resemble one another:

> *He is like a tree planted by streams of water.* (1:3)

(implying that the godly man is sturdy and immovable; other examples: 1:4; 5:12; 17:8)

Metaphor

a comparison in which one thing is declared to be another:

> *For the* LORD *God is a sun and shield.* (84:11)

(implying that God guides and protects; other examples: 23:1; 9:14)

Hyperbole

use of exaggeration to emphasize a point:

> *All night long I flood my bed with weeping.* (6:6)

(implying that the psalmist is deeply saddened; other examples: 78:27; 107:26)

Anthropomorphism

assigning human traits to God's person to convey a truth about God:

> *Turn your ear to me.* (31:2)

> (implying, "Listen to me, Lord"; other examples: 11:4; 18:15; 32:8)

Personification

assigning characteristics of a human to lifeless objects:

> *All my bones say, "LORD, who is like unto thee?"* (35:10, NKJV)

> (implying "I praise you from my innermost being"; other examples: 11:4; 18:15; 32:8)

About the Author

COLONEL HENRY GARIEPY served for fifteen years as National Editor-in-Chief and Literary Secretary for The Salvation Army prior to his retirement in 1995. He now serves as a literary consultant, adjunct college faculty, adult Bible teacher, and Corps Sergeant Major – the Army's chief lay leader – in Toms River, New Jersey.

He is the author of more than twenty books and numerous articles. His *Portraits of Christ* has had a circulation of over 200,000 copies, and, like his *Portraits of Perseverance,* has been published in several editions and languages. His commissioned writings have included the authorized biography of General Eva Burrows (with a foreword by Billy Graham) and Volume 8 of the International History of The Salvation Army.

The author is an outdoor enthusiast and has completed three twenty-six-mile marathons. He earned his Bachelor of Arts and Master of Science degrees in Urban Studies and was honored by his alma mater with its 1994 Alumni Lifetime Leadership Award. He and his wife, Marjorie, take great delight in their four children and twelve grandchildren.